The Search for Spirituality

The Search for Spirituality

Seven Paths within the Catholic Tradition

Edited by Stephen J. Costello

The Liffey Press
Dublin

Published by
The Liffey Press
Ashbrook House
10 Main Street
Raheny, Dublin 5
www.theliffeypress.com

© 2002 Stephen J. Costello and individual contributors

A catalogue record of this book is
available from the British Library.

ISBN 1-904148-23-9

Cover image, "The Beatitudes" by Evie Hone, is
from the Prayer Room, Manresa House,
Jesuit Centre of Spirituality, Dollymount, Dublin 3.
Reproduced with permission.

Printed in the Republic of Ireland by Colour Books Ltd.

CONTENTS

ACKNOWLEDGEMENTS

My profuse thanks goes to the seven contributors in this compilation without whom this book would literally not have been written: Thomas Martin, OSA, Andrew Nugent, OSB, Wilfrid McGreal, OCarm, Nivard Kinsella, OCSO, Aidan Nichols, OP, Francis Cotter, OFM and Joseph Veale, SJ.

I would like also to thank my family for their support, help and interest and my friends for their presence in my life: John Rice, Oisín and Elva Quinn, Darren Cleary, Thomas O'Connor, Bob Haugh, Pat Treacy, Hugh Cummins, Mark and Kelly Coyle, Brigid Ruane, Brendan Dowling, Fr Derek Smyth and Fr John Harris, OP. My admiration and gratitude go also to Fr Terence Hartley, OSB and Abbot Celestine Cullen, OSB. They have helped me in countless ways ever since I began to visit Glenstal Abbey at the age of 18. This book is dedicated to them.

PREFACE

The Search for Spirituality explores the seven main paths within the Catholic tradition: Augustinian, Benedictine, Carmelite, Cistercian, Dominican, Franciscan and Ignatian. It is intended for all those on a search, for all those struggling with meaning, suffering, hoping, hating and loving. It weaves together a tapestry of Catholic Christianity, with each contribution — written by an expert in that particular area — being a thread that connects us to a living historical tradition and a vibrant, sometimes unknown, path of prayer in the present.

A distinction is often drawn between (academic) theology and (lived) spirituality. But though they are distinct, they are not opposed. Spirituality must be rooted in theology and tradition lest it become sentimental and saccharine. Theology should not become divorced from an existential commitment to faith lest it become irrelevant and impotent. Each presupposes and is required by the other. That said, the stress in this book is on spirituality. Every reader will find something in it that will speak to them of ultimate love because it is for this that the human heart longs.

The contributors to the book are Thomas Martin, OSA (Augustinian), Andrew Nugent, OSB (Benedictine), Wilfrid McGreal, OCarm (Carmelite), Nivard Kinsella, OCSO (Cistercian), Aidan Nichols, OP (Dominican), Francis Cotter, OFM (Franciscan) and Joseph Veale, SJ (Jesuit).

There has been an explosion of interest in spirituality of late but much of what is written in the area appears to be too superficial, too assured and easy, even smug, lacking philosophical and theological knowledge and sometimes unaware of tradition and appreciation of historical development. This book attempts to address this myopia. Each article is written by a person who is a "practising" (respectively) Augustinian friar, Benedictine monk, Cistercian monk, Carmelite friar, Dominican friar, Franciscan friar and Jesuit priest. They come from these diverse traditions, are formed in them and so speak out of them. There are Benedictine nuns but there are no Jesuit nuns; there are Carmelite nuns though female Carmelites live enclosed, contemplative lives while their male colleagues live mendicant lives (half monastic, half apostolic). Such are the quirks and peculiarities of the different religious Orders as they have been founded and developed. Each carries its own unique stamp and possesses its own particular missionary objective.

Of course, each contributor, while belonging to a particular Order or Society, is writing from his personal understanding and interpretation of that spirituality and Order or Society. Needless to say, there are other groupings within the penumbra of Catholicism and indeed there are Anglican monastic Orders that do not feature in this collection. Mention could have been made of the Christian Brothers, the Redemptorists, the Oblates, the Vincentians or of the huge host of female religious such as the Mercy, Presentation or Sacred Heart sisters, but what is reflected and represented in this compilation are seven of the major and oldest traditions within the Roman Catholic Church.

As far as I am aware, no other book has sought to synthesise these several strands within a single volume. I thought the idea to be not only worthwhile and interesting to pursue and present, but believe it to be essential for anyone intent on understanding these ancient traditions, rediscovering them anew or simply searching for a path of prayer and spiritual practice. If this work succeeds in fulfilling any of these criteria, it will have been more than worth the endeavour.

ABOUT THE CONTRIBUTORS

Stephen J. Costello, MA, PhD

Born in Dublin, educated at St Gerard's School and Castleknock College, Stephen J. Costello studied philosophy at University College Dublin and subsequently trained in psychoanalysis. He received his Masters degree and Doctorate from the National University of Ireland in philosophy and lectures in philosophy and psychoanalysis at University College Dublin, Trinity College and LSB College. Dr Costello also has a Diploma in Psychoanalytic Psychotherapy and is a member of the Association for Psychoanalysis and Psychotherapy in Ireland and also of the Irish Aikido Association. He is the author of *Basil Hume*: *Builder of Community* (Veritas, 1988), *The Irish Soul*: *In Dialogue* (Liffey Press, Dublin, 2001), and *The Pale Criminal*: *Psychoanalytic Perspectives* (Karnac, London and New York, 2002).

Francis Cotter, OFM

Francis Cotter, OFM, a native of Urlingford, Co. Kilkenny, is a member of the Irish Franciscan Province. After studies in University College Galway and in Rome he was ordained in 1982. He went on to receive an MA in Franciscan Studies from St Bonaventure University, New York, and a doctorate in spiritual theology from the Franciscan Institute, Antonianum, Rome. He has since mainly worked in the formation of young friars in both Rome and Zimbabwe, and is presently living in Dublin.

Nivard Kinsella, OCSO

Fr Nivard was born and educated in Dublin. He entered the Cistercian Community of Mount St Joseph Abbey, Roscrea, where he was professed and ordained priest. He studied in Rome at the Angelicum and took a doctorate in theology there. He spent a couple of years on a monastic foundation from Roscrea, in Australia (Tarrawarra Abbey). He has held various offices in the Community and has lectured in most of the monasteries of the Order in the USA, as well as in Ireland and Britain.

Thomas Martin, OSA, PhD

Thomas F. Martin, OSA is Associate Professor in the Department of Theology and Religious Studies at Villanova University in the United States. He has lectured and published extensively on the thought of St Augustine.

Wilfrid McGreal, ODC

Wilfrid McGreal joined the Carmelite Order at The Friars, Aylesford in 1957. After studies in Rome, Dublin and the University of Kent at Canterbury, he was involved in youth ministry for many years and was also the University Chaplain to London University. Since 1990 he has been a member of the Carmelite Community at Aylesford where he is involved in retreat work, writing and he has taken an active part in ecumenical activity in Kent. He is a frequent broadcaster and is also a regular contributor to various newspapers. Currently, Wilfrid McGreal is the Prior of the Community at Aylesford and is also responsible for organising and caring for the many pilgrimages that take place at The Friars.

Aidan Nichols, OP

Aidan Nichols was born in 1948 in Lytham St Anne's (England) to an Anglican family. He became a Catholic in 1966. After university, he entered the English Dominican Province at Blackfriars, Oxford. Since ordination, he has worked as a student chaplain at Edinburgh and Cambridge, and taught theology at the Angelicum in Rome, Oscott College in Birmingham and Blackfriars in Oxford. At present, he is Prior of Blackfriars Cambridge and an "affiliated lecturer" in the Cambridge Divinity School. He is a prolific writer and the author of numerous scholarly works.

Andrew Nugent, OSB

Born in Dublin in 1937, educated at Blackrock College, UCD and the King's Inns, Andrew Nugent practised as a barrister for some years before entering Glenstal Abbey in Co. Limerick in 1961. He studied theology at Strasbourg University during the heady days of Vatican II and graduated with the Student Revolution of 1968. There followed thirty years in the Abbey boarding school as teacher, housemaster, and Headmaster, punctuated by three incarnations, totalling nearly ten years, in the Glenstal monastic foundation at Ewu-Ishan, Nigeria, where he served as Novice Master and Prefect of Studies, as well as being actively engaged in parish work. Much in demand for retreats, he has written many articles on aspects of pastoral theology and spirituality. He is currently Prior at Glenstal Abbey.

Joseph Veale, SJ

Fr Joseph Veale is a member of the Irish Jesuit Province. He taught English in Gonzaga College. He has regularly given the *Spiritual Exercises* of St Ignatius in Ireland and abroad and has written extensively in the area of Ignatian spirituality. For the past twenty years, he has been a Jesuit spiritual director.

Dedication

This book is dedicated to Abbot Celestine Cullen, OSB and Dom Terence Hartley, OSB, my monastic mentors, with admiration and gratitude.

O after Christmas we'll have no need to go searching
For the difference that sets an old phrase burning —
We'll hear it in the whispered argument of a churning
Or in the streets where the village boys are lurching
And we'll hear it among decent men too
Who burrow dung in gardens under trees,
Wherever life pours ordinary plenty.

— Patrick Kavanagh, "Advent".

INTRODUCTION:
CATHOLIC SPIRITUALITY

Stephen J. Costello

This work is a study in Catholic spirituality. Spirituality is concerned with the human subject in relation to God. Spirituality stresses the relational and the personal though does not neglect the social and political dimensions of a person's relationship to the divine. The distinction between what is to be believed in the domain of dogmatic theology (the *credenda*) and what is to be done as a result of such belief in the domain of moral theology (the *agenda*) is not always clear. Spirituality develops out of moral theology's concern for the *agenda* of the Christian life of faith. Spirituality covers the domain of religious experience of the divine. It is primarily experiential and practical/existential rather than abstract/academic and conceptual. Seven *vias* or ways are included in this compilation and we shall take a

look at each of them in turn, attempting to highlight the
main themes and tenets of these seven spiritual paths.[1]

Augustinian Spirituality

It is probably a necessary tautology to state that Augustinian spirituality derives from the life, works and faith
of the African Saint Augustine of Hippo (354–430).
This spirituality is one of *conversion* to Christ through
caritas. One's ultimate home is in God and our hearts
are restless until they rest in the joy and intimacy of Father, Son and Spirit. We are made for the eternal Jerusalem. The key word here in our earthly pilgrimage is
"conversion" and Augustine describes his own experience of conversion (*metanoia*) biographically in Books
I–IX of his *Confessions*,[2] a spiritual classic, psychologically in Book X (on Memory), and theologically in
Books XI–XIII. Conversion is seen as a call to relationship with Christ through self-transcending love for God
and men alike. Conversion signals *change* and absorp-
tion of the Gospel and its teachings into the practice of
caritas in daily living. That said, Augustinian spirituality has intellectual, moral, mystical, sacramental and
apostolic dimensions. Augustinian spirituality does not
require one to abandon the world but to embrace it, not
to forsake it but to collaborate in its creation and trans-
formation. Through baptism, the three Persons of the
divine Trinity dwell in the soul and the Trinity reveals
itself as the Father caring, the Son being compassionate
and the Spirit loving. The Triune God calls all restless

hearts to live in the very embrace of the Trinity. As such man is *capax Dei* — we all have a capacity for communion with God, a capacity actualised in baptism through which we participate in Trinitarian life. We are made in God's own image and likeness. We long to know and love God — this is the prayer of the human heart. Love arouses desire. And faith seeks understanding. A preparation and purgation or purification of desire is required in order to exhibit and incorporate Trinitarian attitudes. Christ the Physician and Healer is needed as well as His mediation — *Christus medicus* (Christ the Physician) is a frequent theme found in Augustine. Christ's most pronounced virtue was His humility, which is the remedy for Adam's fall through *hubris*.

One prepares for participation in the divine life through a meditative reading of Scripture and through prayer, fasting and good works as the heart becomes purified and filled with agapic love. Through the eye of the heart one begins to see God in His images — in one's self and one's neighbour. Augustine employs the biblical notion of the "heart", as the affective aspect of faith that unites body and spirit. If Christ is the perfect image of the Father, the human person is made in the imperfect image of the Trinity. The search for God should result in a living faith and loving life. The contemplation of God is every Christian's ultimate hope and eternal destiny. Augustine sees the spiritual life as involving the re-formation of the image of the Trinity in the human person through grace. Augustinian spiritual-

ity places much emphasis on the Trinity (as indeed does
St Ignatius).

Augustinian spirituality is founded on the reality of
sanctifying grace. The infused *habitus* in the soul makes
possible a life of union with God as Three Persons in
One and One in Three. Intimacy with the indwelling
Trinity — with the divine Persons — develops by degrees but is strengthened and made possible through a
life of prayer and living out of the beatitudes.

Augustine attempts to describe this ascent to God
from the purgative through the illuminative to the unitive. Seven steps are delineated on the ladder of perfection and piety: 1) fear of God's righteous punishment as
one comes to terms with one's repentance and remorse;
2) meekness in docility to God's commandments and to
Scripture; 3) mourning of one's own inadequacy
through the realisation of the gulf separating man from
God, creature from Creator; 4) thirst for justice; 5)
enlightenment to perform merciful acts; 6) attention to
God; 7) contemplation of God, seeing Him in all things
and all things in Him (which is also a theme running
through Ignatian spirituality).

There are both active/apostolic and contemplative
strands in Augustinian spirituality. Acting and contemplating. Through connaturality, one experiences God in
contemplation. Such contemplative knowledge is experiential.

Grace enables the will to choose the good, according
to Augustine. *Libertas* — (joyful) freedom — is the con-

dition of the perfection of free choice (*liberum arbitrium*). The notion of creaturely freedom and the freedom of the risen life is a recurring motif in Augustine. Through love of God one makes God's will one's own. Hence his biblical exhortation: "love and do as you please".[3] Love is the key to spiritual freedom.

Augustinian monasteries were not founded for a particular purpose like preaching (as with the Dominicans) or teaching but to build up the (Mystical) Body of Christ. Love characterises the Augustinian monastery and Augustinians go out to give this love and so Augustinians became, in time, mendicants. The *Rule of St Augustine* (396–400) is the oldest surviving *Rule* for religious in the West and exemplifies Augustinian spirituality — union with others through union with God. The emphasis in the *Rule* is less on power than on prayer, less on precepts and penances and more on charity and compassion. The Augustinian is not a slave under the law but a person under grace.

The following is a list of those who today live or at least follow the *Rule of St Augustine*: the Hermits of St Augustine dating from the 5th century and united in 1256 into the Order of St Augustine, abbreviated to OSA; the Canons Regular, the Premonstratensians (1120), the Dominicans (1235) and the Servites (1256) also adopted the *Rule*; in the 14th century, it was adopted by both lay and eremitical confraternities; in the 16th century it was adopted by teaching orders, by the Piarists and more recently by the Augustinians of the Assumption of Mary, called the Assumptionists (the 19th century). The following is a list of the female orders who follow the *Rule*: the Bridgettines (1344), Annunciates (1500), Ursulines (1535), Salesian Sisters and the Poor Teaching Sisters of Our Blessed Lady (1833); the Magdalene Sisters of the Middle Ages (1833) and their modern counterparts; the Angelicals of St Paul (1530); the Sisters of Our Lady of Charity of Refuge (1644); and the Daughters of the Good Shepherd (1692). In some countries, there are also contemplative Augustinian nuns. Through the Third Order (for lay people) of the Augustinians, the Servites and the Dominicans, the *Rule* is preserved and practised among laypeople and many other congregations of tertiaries follow suit. There are also the Discalced Augustinians, a 16th century branch who are contemplatives and who became an independent order in 1931. There are also the Augustinian Recollects.

The missionary spirit is alive and well among Augustinians too. Members of the Augustinian family who have been canonised include Augustine's mother, St Monica, and belonging to the Augustinian tradition are St Gregory the Great, St Bernard of Clairvaux, Hugh and Richard of St Victor, amongst others. The Franciscan spirituality of St Bonaventure is Augustinian in its Trinitarian focus and there is a similar affinity between Augustinian spirituality and St Ignatius's mysticism of the inner (Trinitarian) life, as we have said. If one were to summarise Augustinian spirituality in one sentence, it would be this: Augustinian spirituality is centred on the Trinity.

Benedictine Spirituality

The 6th century *Regula Benedicti*, or *Rule of St Benedict*, is the foundation document for most monks in the West though many treatises on Benedictine spirituality also draw on the Life of St Benedict found in the *Dialogues* of Gregory the Great and on Benedict's *Regula Magistri* or *The Rule of the Master*, which emphasises anchoretic spirituality and the cenobitic masters such as Basil and Augustine. The spiritual core of the *Rule of St Benedict* has inspired Christians for fifteen centuries.

Benedict's God is an exalted one; nowhere is the name of Jesus ever mentioned in the *Rule*, nor is a historical event of His life recorded, except the crucifixion on the Cross. For the Benedictine monk, God is very much present at the monastic liturgy of the Divine Office and so every aspect of its performance is carried out with meticulous concern and care.

A Benedictine monastery is directed to one end — the search for God — and five times a day the monks file into church to sing Psalms to God: at Matins, at Lauds (sometimes conjoined), at the midday Office, at Mass, at Vespers and Compline. The abbey church is central to community life as the God of the Benedictines is hymned in lovely Latin cadences. "Listen, my brothers, I have something to tell you. I have a way of life to teach you." These are the opening words of the *Rule of St*

Benedict and Benedictines follow this *Rule* by taking vows of obedience, stability and "conversion of manners" (*Conversio Morum*), which implies a life of frugality and chastity. Monks withdraw into the desert to ponder the mystery that is God. Learn it there and the monk will have something to sell in the market place — the pearl of great price. Silence is cultivated as the soul meets God deep within its own interiority. A Benedictine monastery is a place of silence. Such "places of silence; deserts where we can meet God in solitude",[4] in the words of the late Basil Hume, himself a Benedictine monk, are essential. Monasteries are places of spiritual energy; they are pointers to prayer. They are spiritual storehouses. A monk is "one alone"; he is a man of prayer and a man of God and a monastery is a house of God. Basil Hume once said that:

> . . . there should be in every [Benedictine] monk a potential Trappist, a potential Carthusian — or, to put it this way — there should be a little regret in each of us that God did not call us to be a Carthusian: a regret that this great vocation was not offered to us.[5]

Just as there should be a disappointed Carmelite in every Sacred Heart sister.

For St Benedict, the abbot, as the superior of the monastery, is the person in whom the divine presence is concentrated — the will of God comes through the abbot. The abbot occupies the place of Christ; his sovereignty extends in the realm of faith and not power politics. The abbatial office is a kind of divine icon. The monks have the right to elect their own abbot. God is to be met, however, in all persons, even in the most pre-possessing ones. Each guest is to be welcomed as Christ; hence the important function of the Guestmaster, through whom all guests come to the monastery.

Like St Francis, Benedict treats creation with reverence, as it reflects and is penetrated by ubiquitous divinity. There is no talking at table lest the Word of God become inaudible — the amount of food and drink is left to discretion and custom. Benedict sees monastic life as one of arduous spiritual striving, even as hard labour. The novice strenuously seeks God. There are un-Augustinian expressions of synergism (co-operation between human and divine) in the *Rule*. But nothing is to be preferred other than Christ, as He preferred nothing to us. The monk ascends the ladder of humility through ascetic effort and God's grace.

In the face of the Almighty, the monk experiences reverential awe; Benedict wants to inculcate reverence as a basic monastic virtue and religious sentiment (together with discretion). Reverence characterises all genuine religious experience of the divine. In silence, the monk is mindful of his God — reverence in relation to God and humility in relation to self. Signs of humility are manifest in tears of compunction, according to Benedict in the *Rule*, which also features in other mediaeval monastic texts. However, Benedict thinks that joy should be present in a Benedictine monastery; a grim atmosphere should not prevail. Joy as a spiritual state, rather than (mere) happiness,[6] ought to predominate. Sadness, as spiritual despair rather than psychological depression, is not counselled by Benedict. Murmuring is cautioned against in Benedictine monk-priests. Benedictine monks are serene. Love is central to both the Christian and the monk; all Christian and monastic virtues are subsumed under the rubric of love and Benedict devotes the penultimate chapter of his *Rule* precisely to this topic. The love that is preached by Benedict is not romantic or idealistic love but one that is manifested in the interpersonal virtues of respect, patience, obedience, selflessness, etc. These are cultivated in community life, although Benedictines have private rooms and expansive social space. A monk needs to preserve a nostalgia for the desert and not seek to be distracted from it — for life lessons are to be learnt there. Internal silence needs to be cultivated.

In a booklet entitled *Basil Hume: Builder of Community*,[7] I wrote:

> *A monastic calling is an exploration of the mystery that is God. It is a search for an experience of his reality. . . . A monastery is a place of silence, a desert where the monks can meet God.*

It is a place where one labours in love. One Irish Benedictine monk in an interview described a monastery to me thus:

> . . . *a monastery is a connecting link, a*
> *powerhouse. . . . The purpose of the monastery*
> *is to be there, like the watchman waiting for the*
> *dawn. You are waiting and listening especially.*
> *It's like the secret service; you're listening for*
> *the instructions for the next part of the*
> *salvation plan.*[8]

The word *infirmus* ("weakness") appears 22 times in
the *Rule*. Benedict was aware that infirmity or weakness
is in ample supply in the monastery. Monks are not perfect — they strive towards perfection, as they seek God,
peacefully. Obedience (etymologically, "obedience"
means "listening to") is required of all the monks, in
contradistinction to a slothful and sinful disobedience
— obedience to the Gospel of love, to the *Rule* and to
the abbot. God speaks to the Benedictine monk through
the abbot and the community, through Scripture, tradition and the magisterium. The *Rule* does not recom-
mend a self-denying asceticism. The Benedictine
horarium does not break the night with prayer. The
Benedictine approach is balanced and based on mod-
eration and order. Their form of prayer rotates around
the *lectio Divina* and especially the Psalms of the Divine
Office. Monks meditate and ruminate on the Word.
Lectio Divina and Gregorian chant is a particularly
Benedictine way of praying. Benedictine spirituality derives ultimately from the *Rule of St Benedict*, which is
one of the classic statements of monastic Christianity in

the West, and has stimulated countless Christians and
seekers down the centuries.

Carmelite Spirituality

The name Carmelite comes from the mountain range
Mount Carmel in the Holy Land, where the Carmelite
Order originated in about 1200 AD. A group of lay her-
mits received a formula of life from Albert, Patriarch of
Jerusalem, between 1206 and 1214, which provided the
Carmelites with their basic spiritual orientation in the
Church. The themes of the formula were solitude (individual cells around a chapel), silence, prayer (chiefly the
Psalms), with a life centred on Christ. The deterioration
of the kingdom made it imperative that the Carmelites
emigrated, which they did, travelling westward in 1238
to Cyprus, Sicily, Southern France and England. They
found that their eremitical life was ill-suited to contemporary religious life in Europe when the Dominicans
and Franciscans were successfully meeting the pastoral
challenges laid down by the Fourth Lateran Council.
The Carmelites received from Innocent IV approval for
some slight changes in the wording of their formula of
life. Under Pope Innocent the formula became an official *Rule* and the Carmelites became friars. This once
semi-eremitic community became more cenobitic.
Formerly Carmelite hermits became mendicant friars
alongside the Dominicans and Franciscans and by the
end of the 13th century the Carmelites were established
in the universities at Cambridge, Oxford and Paris.

They were now a major mendicant order in the Catholic Church. Their constitution was modelled on the Dominican Order and their spirituality, in turn, mirrored this move: mobility instead of monastic stability, corporate as well as personal poverty, modified monastic prayers and practices and a commitment to pastoral ministry. In the 13th century, their former eremitical monasticism was fully replaced by a cenobitic mendicancy in response to contemporary circumstances. This reform created the tension within Carmelite spirituality — solitude and community. It is a tension present in all mendicant orders.

Elijah, the Prophet, occupies a privileged place in Carmelite spirituality as he had been adopted as a paradigm and model for monks, especially for hermits. When the Carmelites settled on Mount Carmel, they were aware of this association and the fountain at their original hermitage on Mount Carmel was later identified as the fountain of Elijah. Elijah may be regarded as an archetype (to use a Jungian term) of Carmelite spirituality and when the French Discalced Carmelites consulted C.G. Jung, he informed and assured them that Elijah was a genuine and living archetype. Elijah has shaped Carmelite consciousness. The fact that the Carmelites had no charismatic founder of the stature of Dominic or Francis or Ignatius led them to emphasising Elijah (from the Hebrew Scriptures) and Mary (from the Christian Scriptures).

The chapel at Mount Carmel was dedicated to Mary and since the 13th century the Carmelites have borne the title of "Brothers of the Blessed Virgin Mary of Mount Carmel". The wearing of the brown scapular, which became widespread in the 19th and early 20th centuries, became a sign of dedication to Mary and is still practised by members of the first, second and third Carmelite orders, as well as among those who belong to the Confraternity of Our Lady of Mount Carmel. Carmelite identity has thus been shaped by a consciousness of the Blessed Virgin.

Second only to the *Rule*, the most important mediaeval text in Carmelite spirituality was the *Institution of the First Monks* (1370) by Philip Ribot, the Provincial of Catalonia. It was a text that was studied by both Teresa of Avila and John of the Cross; it laid the groundwork for the mystical orientation of Carmelite spirituality that would come to fruition in the work and lives of these two outstanding saints and in the Tourain Reform (there was also the Mantuan Reform in the 15th century). It is an important document for anyone intent on or interested in understanding the roots of the Carmelite contemplative tradition.

The most significant reform in the Carmelite Order came through the conversion experience of a nun at the Carmelite monastery of the Incarnation in Avila. It was a catalyst for sweeping changes. Teresa of Jesus, as she was then called, composed *The Way of Perfection* in response to the requests of her nuns for instruction in prayer. She also penned the *Book of Foundations* and wrote her *Life* for her confessors. But her classic work describing the mystical journey to God is *The Interior Castle*, which details the seven mansions — the first three being a prelude to the mystical life, the last four being the journey to the mystical union of spiritual marriage. She gives voice here to the Carmelite contemplative tradition. Her reforms, after the death of John of the Cross, led to the creation of the Discalced Carmelites. Teresa of Avila (1515–1582), as she is now known, was canonised in 1622 and in 1970 she was declared the first woman Doctor of the Church.

She chose a friar to help her in her work of reform, whom history knows as St John of the Cross (1542–1591). It was while he was locked up that he composed many of the stanzas of his "Spiritual Canticle". He has left us with four commentaries: *The Spiritual Canticle*, *The Living Flame of Love*, *The Dark Night* (the "dark night of the soul", what the Jesuits call the God of "desolation", being almost synonymous with the name of John of the Cross) and *The Ascent of Mount Carmel*. The Spanish poets of the 20th century did much to popularise the poetry of John of the Cross. The writings of both John of the Cross and Teresa of Avila are classical statements of Carmelite spirituality. John of the Cross was canonised in 1726 and declared a Doctor of the Church in 1926.

Alongside Teresa of Avila and John of the Cross, the next most widely known Carmelite is Saint Thérèse of

Lisieux (1873–1897). Her designation as the "little
flower" derives from her love of flowers and her self-
depiction as a little flower. She lived and wrote about
spirituality in the crucible of suffering — she experienced a terrible, haunting darkness for the last 18
months of her life and admitted that it was her faith
that protected against suicide. The sources of her spirituality were the Bible, especially the Gospels, the *Imitation of Christ* and the writings of John of the Cross. Her
Story of a Soul is similarly a spiritual classic.

   A modern Carmelite figure is Edith Stein (1891–
1942), a Jew who converted to Catholicism and subsequently became a Carmelite nun in her native Germany.
She was a brilliant philosopher, being at one time the
assistant to Edmund Husserl (as Heidegger would be
too), founder of phenomenology. She was to be exe-
cuted by the Nazis (of which Heidegger was a sup-
porter) at Auschwitz concentration camp. She was
beatified in 1987.

   To conclude: originally Carmelite spirituality developed from the Mount Carmel hermits with their emphasis on solitude and prayer but a pastoral orientation
was introduced in the middle of the 13th century when
the Carmelite Order became a mendicant one; equally
influential on the evolution of Carmelite spirituality has
been the contributions of the cloistered Carmelite nuns.
Anyone wishing to further explore Carmelite spirituality
is referred to the writings of John of the Cross and
Teresa of Avila.

Cistercian Spirituality

The Cistercian Order takes its name from the mother abbey, Cîteaux, founded in Burgundy in 1098 as a reform of Benedictine monasticism. Today, the Cistercian Order is divided into two main groups: the Order of Cîteaux (OCist); and the Cistercian Order of the Strict Observance (OCSO) or Trappists.

Attempts at reform and renewal of monastic life were made during the 11th century under Pope Gregory VII. A new interpretation of the possibilities inherent in the *Rule of St Benedict* was underway and an attempt was made to recover the integrity of the *Rule*. Those gathered at the monastery in Cîteaux tried to live by the *Rule* in a literal fashion, distancing themselves from the customs and conventions derived from Cluny and other traditional Benedictine centres. The desire was for poverty and seclusion: to be "poor with the poor Christ". Poverty was a priority. This simplicity was seen in the liturgy and was reflected in its radically simplified ritual. The monks did not run schools and contact with the outside world was kept to a minimum. Nonetheless, the Cistercians developed an integral and influential monastic culture. A distinguished form and style of architecture emerged that combined austerity with space and simplicity with proportion; arts and skills evolved and techniques of sanitation and agriculture were developed.

The Golden Age of Cistercian history can be dated from 1098 to 1250 when their influence was at a peak. We may mention St Bernard of Clairvaux (1090–1153),

who is one of the great contemplative Doctors of the
Church. A revival in scholarly interest in Bernard was
seen in 1940 with the publication of Etienne Gilson's
The Mystical Theology of Saint Bernard. Jean
Leclercq, OSB, of Clairvaux also contributed to Bernar-
dine research with his co-editing of the critical works.
Bernard's work may be seen as a monastic theology, as
a monastic response to Revelation. Bernard was optimistic with regard to salvation and confident in grace.
Human beings *by nature* desire God. Bernard was
much taken by the Augustinian theme of *desire for God*
(which is also an Ignatian theme).

The historical development of the Cistercian Order
chronicles and charts its change away from monasticism in the direction of education and outside involvement. This was in part due to external circumstances
such as the Black Death, which decimated many monasteries, and the decline in religious fervour generally.
Many Cistercian houses assumed responsibilities for
schools and parishes. In France, though, there was a
counter-movement toward a more austere lifestyle,
which divided the Order into "Common Observance",
which was more oriented to priestly work and education, and "Strict Observance", which sought to curtail
such activities and concentrate more on a contemplative way of life, with the most effective and efficient of
the reformers being the Abbot of La Trappe (his followers were to receive the name of "Trappist").

The most significant modern monastic was the 20th century Cistercian, Thomas Merton, whose autobiography, *The Seven Storey Mountain*, became a bestseller.[9] Though the numbers entering the Cistercian Order have declined since the Second Vatican Council, there is evidence of some regrowth in Europe and the United States. Such an Order will always appeal to those in search of a more authentic community life and with an interest in unceasing prayer within the cell of silence.

Like the Cistercians, the Carthusians also draw their inspiration from the *Rule of St Benedict*. The Carthusians were founded by St Bruno (1032–1101) whose words were: "God and God alone, in solitude". The monastic literature of that time valued the writings of Augustine, Basil, the Desert Fathers and the *Conferences* of John Cassian. From the Cistercians, the Carthusians received the writings of St Bernard. Carthusians seek to live austere, hidden lives of prayer and wear the white habit as a sign of devotion to Our Lady.

Carthusians prefer places apart in rugged, well-wooded mountainous terrains where they can be silent and still with their God — a place apart but a life together. In such solitude, they study and pray — "o blessed solitude". They live in the silence of their cell where they pass the greater part of their lives. Carthusian spiritual discipline creates space for the monk "to cultivate the cell". Becoming empty, being still and attentively listening is the silent work of the cell whose prayer is for continual, uninterrupted union with God.

Dominican Spirituality

Dominican Spirituality is the legacy of the Order of Preachers (OP), which was founded by St Dominic (1170–1221). It is a religious family comprising friars, nuns and sisters and has provided the world with a plethora of saints including three Doctors of the Church: Albert the Great (ca. 1200–1280), Thomas Aquinas (ca. 1225–1274), and Catherine of Siena (1347–1380).

At the time of Dominic, preaching was the privilege of the bishops alone but Pope Innocent III supported the new approach taken by St Dominic and in 1206 he granted Dominic the right to preach. From that date on, Dominic signed himself as "Brother Dominic, Preacher". Dominic and his followers adopted the *Rule of St Augustine* and the title "Order of Preachers" was recognised in 1217. A year later, Dominic dispersed some of his friars to Paris and Bologna where priories were established at the homes of the two major universities of mediaeval Europe. The Dominicans prioritise (the apostolate of) preaching; they live a common life with choral Office, with the emphasis on study and contemplation. Saints Benedict, Francis and Augustine left a *Rule* and a model of life while Dominic left a task — the task of preaching the Gospel truth. A life in common, liturgy, contemplation and study were to be combined and blended together into a whole. The love of God and neighbour were two sides of a single love. Dominican life is thus a mixture of the monastic and the active apostolate — it is truly mendicant.

In a Dominican priory, liturgical life is centred on the choral celebration of the Divine Office and Mass but the Office, unlike with the Benedictines, is celebrated in brevity lest study and preaching be impeded. Dominican Gregorian chant is simpler than its Benedictine counterpart. Dominic exhorts not a method of prayer but proffers the idea of the engagement of the whole person while praying — body and soul, reason as well as emotions (as indeed does Ignatius). Due to its emphasis on preaching, Dominican spirituality may be regarded as a spirituality of the Word incarnate. And study, as the *Constitutions* make clear, is for the sake of preaching. A theologian is thus a person of prayer first and foremost. Theology must culminate in adoration. Dominicans are not content merely to acquire knowledge but experientially to penetrate the mysteries of faith through reason. Dominican friars highly value the contributions of philosophy, especially the philosophy deriving from the Dominican Thomas Aquinas (*viz,* Thomism). Though history recalls Dominicans being overcome with (misguided) zeal in their efforts to defend the orthodoxy at the time of the Spanish Inquisition (it is difficult to imagine a Benedictine presiding over a burning fire), Dominic himself devoted much of his private prayer time to petition for the salvation of souls, as his canonisation process makes plain.

Though there were no Dominican spiritual writers until the 14th century, Dominicans wrote biblical commentaries and Dominic himself highly valued the works

of Cassian and Bernard of Clairvaux as well as the
Church Fathers. Even with the rise of Scholasticism,
spirituality and theology were not seen as strictly separate and in St Thomas spirituality becomes expressed in
theology.

St Thomas Aquinas provided the Dominicans with
their most famous and influential figure in philosophy
and theology. Aquinas penned his famous *Summa
Theologiae* most likely for his confreres in the priories.
To this day, Thomism is the official philosophy of the
Catholic Church. If intellect is primary for Aquinas, he
is also of the opinion that love flows from knowledge.
Aquinas adopted the Aristotelian position that the soul
is the form of the body, in contradistinction to Platonic
dualism. He also gives five "proofs" for the existence of
God. His influence in philosophy cannot be overstated.

After the death of Aquinas and the condemnation of
some propositions associated with his teaching, the
hegemony resided with the Franciscans Duns Scotus
and William of Ockham.[10] For some, the intellectualism
and optimism of Aquinas were seen as a threat to God's
freedom. Meister Eckhart (ca. 1260–1328) sought to
combine the teaching of Thomas with German mysticism. Eckhart was influenced by Thomas but also by
Bernard of Clairvaux, Maimonides, the Pseudo-
Dionysius and neo-Platonism. He held that in the spark
of the soul, in the seat of divine life, we are equal to
God. This led to charges of heresy being brought against

him in Cologne and a number of his propositions were also condemned.

Catherine of Siena, a lay Dominican born in 1347, more than any other Dominican (except Dominic himself), exemplifies the Dominican dynamic and dialectic of action and contemplation. She emphasises knowledge and love. (Knowledge begetting love was Aquinas' insight.) The pursuit of truth, centred on liturgy and a life in common, nourished by prayer and preaching is the hallmark of the Dominican way of life and continues to inspire the Dominicans of the 20th century, among whom we can mention Chenu, Congar and Schillebeeckx, all of whom have combined work and scholarship with contemplation and silence.

Franciscan Spirituality

Franciscan spirituality takes its inspiration and mandate from the life and works of Francis and Clare of Assisi. Shortly before his death, St Francis of Assisi (1182–1226) dictated his *Testament* and in so doing left his followers a blueprint for Franciscan living. In his *Testament*, Francis identified the first moment of his spiritual life with an encounter with a leper. This was to mark the rest of his life — in this meeting, the rich young merchant came face to face with human misery. Subsequently, he began to live a life of prayer and penance. This experience of grace established Franciscan spirituality as involving the poor and crucified Christ. This resulted in Francis's move from the communal life

of Assisi to life at the margins of that society, with the
poor and powerless, the lepers and the lonely. The *Legend of Perugia* is a source that contains eyewitness ac-
counts of Francis by his early companions and depicts
his life of prayer, poverty, humility, simplicity, frugality
and fraternity. Indeed, these were to become the hall-
marks of Franciscan spirituality. The Franciscan *Rule*
received papal confirmation in 1223. Franciscan life
emphasises relationships of brotherhood and sisterhood in imitation of Christ our Brother.

St Francis received the stigmata in September 1224.
The stigmata can be seen as the fruit on Francis's flesh
of his focus on the mystery of Christ. Francis's compassion for all of creation including animals has frequently
been commented upon, especially those things in which
an allegorical similarity to the Son of God may be found
— lambs, flowers, worms even. Francis celebrates cosmic creation. For Francis, the created world is a reconciled space in fraternity. In his *Letter to the Entire
Order*, written two years before his death, Francis
communicates his vision of Franciscan life. The mission
is one of praise to the Creator. Creation is gift and God
is fraternal. Through Christ, all men and women are
reconciled and united in a common brotherhood and
sisterhood — creation itself is fraternal. Contemporary
concern with issues of peace and justice, environment
and inter-religious dialogue are all integral aspects of
Franciscan spirituality (recent Generals of the Jesuits
have likewise conjoined faith with social justice). It is a

life of continual conversion involving a concrete turning towards others, to lepers, to the poor, to animals and outcasts and to all of creation itself.

Clare of Assisi (1194–1253) followed the example set by St Francis. She became the first female member of the Franciscan Order — she was both follower of Francis and foundress in her own right and was canonised in 1255. The Poor Clares were originally called the Poor Sisters and attempted to live out the poverty as well as the goodness and generosity of Francis. Clare was initially forced to accept the *Rule of St Benedict* due to regulations laid down in the Fourth Lateran Council convoked by Pope Innocent III governing the rules of religious life, but as she lay on her deathbed her *Rule* was approved by Innocent IV. Poverty was to be respected because poverty creates sisterhood, according to Clare. In holding fast to the footprints of Christ in poverty, one is joined as sister to Christ as spouse. Christ as man was the lowest of men — despised, struck, scourged, suffering and ultimately crucified on a Cross. The poverty of his earthly life and the charity of His Passion were suspended on the wood of the Cross. Such a contemplation of the crucified Christ takes place for the Poor Clares within an enclosure that expresses concretely this love of poverty and life of love.

The Franciscan tradition and Franciscan spirituality have developed from these two charismatic figures but is also nurtured by others in the Franciscan family, including St Bonaventure, who adumbrated the Franciscan vision and journey in his classic work, *The Soul's Journey into God*. Francis's own life journey is reflected theologically in Bonaventure's work: from the created world that bears Trinitarian traces, to an understanding of human identity in the poor and crucified Christ, culminating in a union with God (which Francis achieved in the stigmata). Bonaventure outlined six stages in his Franciscan spiritual path, from the created world, to the human person, to affective union with God through Christ crucified. Bonaventuran Christocentric mysticism is mirrored and modelled on the life and experience of Francis himself. Bonaventure exhorts his readers to picture Christ on the Cross. This is a Franciscan method of visual meditation.

We may also mention John Duns Scotus, who died in 1308, as another theologian and philosopher whose uniquely Franciscan approach to the predestination of Christ, Mary's Immaculate Conception and the primacy of love also directly reflects Francis's spiritual intuitions. For Duns Scotus, creation is marked and loved by God for its very "thisness". The influence of Franciscans on the Golden Age of Spanish mysticism in the 16th century has been profound. Franciscan spirituality is one of human liberation whose consistent focus is on the poor, suffering, crucified Christ.

Ignatian Spirituality

St Ignatius of Loyola (1491–1556) founded the Society of Jesus (SJ), also known as the Jesuits. Ignatius was a soldier who sustained an injury to his leg while defending a fortress against French forces in Pamplona in Northern Spain. During his recuperation, he read a number of religious works and experienced a religious conversion, after which he decided to dedicate his life to Christ. He set out on a pilgrimage to the famous Benedictine monastery of Montserrat and, after, departed for Manresa. The time he spent there was the most important in his life — Ignatius the knight became Ignatius the hermit. In his lifetime, he experienced visions and other otherworldly phenomena of Christ, the Trinity and Our Lady. He gathered a group of "companions" (as they were called) together — the Society of Jesus — that became a renowned religious family. He established colleges, universities and was deeply concerned about the poor, the sick and the education of the young. He wrote the *Constitutions* of the Society and the hugely influential *Spiritual Exercises*, which is his classic contribution to the spiritual life. It contains many of the things he experienced by the Cardoner river, a mile from Manresa.[11] Ignatius grounds his contemplative insights in the soil of his Christology.

In one particular vision at La Sorta near Rome, God put Ignatius with Christ to serve and promised Ignatius and his followers that he would be favourable to them in Rome. Ignatius' union with the Triune God fostered a community of love in service to the Pope. Ignatian spirituality is thus communal, ecclesial, Christocentric, papal, priestly and Eucharistic. Ignatian spirituality

significantly shaped Catholic spirituality after the 16th
century. It influenced Jesuits, men and women of other
religious orders and all those who have come in contact
with this radical, innovative path of prayer and spiritual
practice.

Ignatian spirituality ultimately derives from the person, Ignatius of Loyola, whose spirituality is profoundly
Trinitarian. He experienced the Essence of inner Trinitarian life — the divine community united in love.
Ignatian spirituality is incarnational, encountering God
in all things and seeing all things in God; it is also kataphatic. Kataphatic theology is "positive" while apophatic theology is "negative". The former attributes
positive qualities to God (for example, His Goodness
etc.), the latter prefers to say that God is better known
by knowing what He is not (the *via negativa*, which is
more Carmelite perhaps). We can only say that God is
not *what* He is in apophatic theology. Ignatian spirituality does not separate love of God, neighbour and the
world. It is Easter spirituality, in that it loves the world
because the Trinitarian God created the world, redeems
and loves it. Jesuits strive to be contemplatives in action. Their spirituality is incarnate — it is one of apostolic service, one that includes rather than ignores the
world in its socio-political dimensions.

The *Exercises* are the manual of prayer for the Society of Jesus and for all those who seek out Ignatian
spirituality for themselves. They are to be experienced
by the one making them; they are not to be read as if

they were a novel. There is an ongoing dialogue between the person making the *Exercises* (the exercitant) and the person giving or directing them (the spiritual director). They consist of contemplations and meditations on Christ's life, death and Resurrection and are organised into four "weeks" (not chronologically, however). The first week corresponds to the purgative way, the second week to the illuminative, the third and fourth to the unitive. A spiritual exercise is a method of meditation, of contemplation, of examination of one's conscience, of mental and vocal prayer. At the heart of the *Exercises* is the question of *desire* — man's desire for God and God's desire (yes, desire) for us. Ignatian spirituality is versatile and individual; it attempts to dispose of disordered desire and attachment and to enable the person to see God in all things and to seek His will. They are adapted to a person's age, attitude, education, etc. — in fact the *Exercises* teach almost 20 different ways of praying. The five themes that structure the *Exercises* are: Creation, Mankind, The Kingdom of God, Christ, The Trinity.

Two claims are made by Ignatius: firstly, that we can find God's will for us, and secondly, that God will communicate His will/desire for us, as creature deals directly with Creator and Creator with creature. Some people have stressed the fact that Ignatian spirituality is a "service" spirituality rather than a "bridal" type of spirituality. Certainly, it is Theocentric; creatures are seen as traces of God and ordered, as such, to Him.

It is perhaps wrong to say that Ignatius subordinated contemplation to service — he felt that one could be a contemplative even in the midst of activity, all for the greater glory of God (*ad majorem Dei gloriam*). What defines Ignatian spirituality is the integration of the personal interior life with the sacramental and liturgical life of the Church. Ignatian spirituality has a strong empirical thrust to it and a solid scriptural, doctrinal and Marian dimension. It comprises both the affective (which must always be effective) and the intellectual aspects of the person.[12]

To conclude, Ignatian spirituality emphasises the will of God, looks to find God everywhere and insists on service to the world and to the being of the Trinitarian God. Modern Jesuits take a "preferential option for the poor" and by so doing faith is inextricably linked with justice. Their prayer life is mostly private rather than communal. The Society of Jesus is one of the largest religious orders within the Catholic Church. Since the time of its inception, it has exerted its own unique and often controversial charisma, and its contribution to education, "liberation" (as in liberation theology), theology, literature, academic life, philosophy and spirituality has been as immense as it has been important, as culturally relevant as it has been spiritually revitalising.[13]

Notes

1   Much of this information is taken from Michael Downey, 1993. My thanks to Dom Andrew Nugent, OSB, for bringing this book to my attention and to Fr Joe Veale, SJ, for making this book available to me in Milltown.

2   Augustine, 1992.

3   *On the Epistle of John 7:8.*

4   Hume, 1979, page 33.

5   Hume, 1979, page 108.

6   See my forthcoming book, *The Philosophy of Happiness.*

7   Costello, 1988, page 13.

8   Costello, 2001, page 117.

9   Mott, 1984.

10   Fremantle, 1954.

11   Meissner, 1992.

12   Sheldrake, 1991.

13   Letson, Higgins, 1996; Loyola, (1989).

References

Augustine (1992), *Confessions*, trans. Henry Chadwick, Oxford and New York: Oxford University Press.

Costello, Stephen (1988), *Basil Hume: Builder of Community*, Dublin: Veritas.

Costello, Stephen (2001), *The Irish Soul: In Dialogue*, Dublin: The Liffey Press.

Downey, Michael (editor) (1993), *The New Dictionary of Catholic Spirituality*, Collegeville, Minnesota: The Liturgical Press.

Fremantle, Anne (1954), *The Age of Belief: The Medieval Philosophers*, New York and Toronto: Mentor Books.

Hume, Basil (1979), *Searching for God*, London: Hodder and Stoughton.

Letson, Douglas and Higgins, Michael (1996), *The Jesuit Mystique*, London: Fount.

Loyola, Ignatius of (1989), *The Spiritual Exercises of Saint Ignatius*, trans. Anthony Mottola, New York, London, Toronto, Sydney, Auckland: Image Books, Doubleday.

Meissner, SJ, W.W. (1992), *The Psychology of a Saint: Ignatius of Loyola*, New Haven: Yale University Press.

Mott, Michael (1984), *The Seven Mountains of Thomas Merton*, London: Sheldon Press.

Sheldrake, SJ, Philip (editor) (1991), *The Way of Ignatius of Loyola: Contemporary Approaches to the Spiritual Exercises*, The Institute of Jesuit Sources.

1

AUGUSTINIAN SPIRITUALITY

Thomas F. Martin, OSA

The very Way has come to you: rise and walk (s. 141.4)[1]

Augustine of Hippo (354–430) is, without doubt, one of the most important spiritual writers within Western Christianity. He emerged at a key moment in the development of the Latin Tradition and with his strength of thought and pen profoundly shaped subsequent theology and spirituality. His corpus of writings extends to some five million words, a quantity unmatched by any ancient writer come down to us. Three of his works — *The Confessions, The Trinity,* and *The City of God* — remain unrivalled; any single one of them would have marked him as a spiritual master. Born of a Christian mother Monnica, subsequently revered as a saint like her son, and a pagan father Patricius, the young Augustine showed genius that was allowed to develop. He left his native Africa for Italy, in search of wealth and success, and eventually became

Imperial Rhetor in Milan. All the while, he felt a deep
and unsatisfied yearning within. In the process he went
through spiritual crisis after spiritual crisis: joining a
controversial sect called the Manichaeans; becoming a
philosophical sceptic; finding a way to truth with the
Platonists (whom we now call "neo-Platonists"); encountering Ambrose the Bishop; and turning to the
writings of St Paul. All these steps paved the way for his
conversion — after St Paul's, one of the best known in
Christianity. He recounted it memorably at the end of
Book Eight of the *Confessions*:

> *And suddenly I heard a voice from some nearby
> house, a boy's voice or a girl's voice, I do not
> know: but it was a sort of sing-song, repeated
> again and again, "Pick it up! Read! Pick it up!
> Read!" . . . Damming back the flood of my tears
> I arose, interpreting the incident as quite cer-
> tainly a divine command to open my book of
> Scripture and read the passage at which I should
> open. . . . So I was moved to return to the place
> where Alypius was sitting, for I had put down
> the Apostle's book there when I arose. I snatched
> it up, opened it, and in silence read the passage
> upon which my eyes fell: "Not in dissipation and
> drunkenness, nor in debauchery and lewdness,
> nor in arguing and jealousy; but put on the Lord
> Jesus Christ, and make no provision for the flesh
> or the gratification of our desires" (Rm. 13:13–
> 14). I had no wish to read further, and no need.
> For in that instant, with the very ending of the
> sentence, it was as if a light of utter confidence*

> *penetrated my heart, and all the darkness of*
> *uncertainty vanished away (conf. 8.12.29).*

Subsequently he abandoned his professional career and became a dedicated servant of God, a *servus Dei*. In Augustine's Christian world this term designated a lay ascetic, someone committed to continence, prayer, and an evangelical life — what we might call a *monk* today but at this point in history without many formal institutional associations. Augustine thought this was the end of his "public life," in fact, he wanted it so to be. But he recounts how God had other intentions:

> *Filled with terror by my sins and my load of*
> *misery I had been turning over in my mind a*
> *plan to flee into solitude, but you forbade me,*
> *and strengthened me by your words. "To this*
> *end Christ died for all," you reminded me, "that*
> *they who are alive may live not for themselves,*
> *but for him who died for them" (2 Cor. 5.15).*
> *See, then, Lord: I cast my care upon you that I*
> *may live, and I will contemplate the wonders*
> *you have revealed . . . I am mindful of my ran-*
> *som. I eat it, I drink it, I dispense it to others . . .*
> *(10.43.69).*[2]

Augustine was ordained priest unexpectedly, eventually became Bishop of Hippo, and then devoted the final four decades of his life to preaching, teaching, and writing. As he lay dying, Roman North Africa was being overrun by Vandal armies, his own port town was under siege, and Augustine's fame had already spread world-wide. It is important to keep in mind this life-journey of Augustine, since the volume of writings he left behind are inseparable from the way he lived. In these writings, in so many ways, he sought to make sense of an experience which he was convinced was neither unique nor solitary. To talk about the Augustinian Way is not only to talk about the Way he teaches, but especially the Way he himself traversed.

So you want to walk: I am the Way (Jo. ev. tr. 22.8)

It ought to be obvious, yet it is too easily forgotten, that the "Augustinian Way" is ever and always the Way of Christ, the *via Christi*. Augustine's journey, both the one he made and the one he taught to others, was *the Christ journey* — this was his own deepest conviction. Augustine so takes Christ for granted as the foundation of his preaching and teaching that, surprisingly, it is possible for us his readers to lose sight of it. He wrote no specific treatise "on Christ" — yet the question and meaning of Christ is immediately below the surface of every great argument or position Augustine is known for: grace and original sin, for example, are fundamentally Christological questions for him. There is a deeply personal and original dimension to Augustine's teaching of the Way of Christ, since it is formed by his own encounter with Christ the Way. Nonetheless, it is acutely sensitive to what the Church holds and teaches concerning Christ.

Augustine's call to public ministry, first as priest and then as bishop, took place when the entire Christian Church still sharply felt the painful theological turmoil that rocked it in the aftermath of the Council of Nicaea in 325, what scholars today call the Arian Controversy. It began as a theological dispute regarding how to understand the divinity of the Son of God, but quickly went to foundational concerns regarding monotheism, salvation, the Bible, the nature of the Church and holiness, and more. By Augustine's day, these concerns were "resolved" but there still was a serious concern for orthodoxy: one must believe and understand Jesus Christ, Son of God and Son of Man, *Deus homo* (a favourite expression of Augustine), according to sound doctrine. As personal and original as Augustine's teaching of the Way of Christ may be, it is ever attentive to this Rule of Faith.

For Augustine, the Way of Christ is first and foremost the way the Son of God himself traversed: the way of Incarnation and Redemption. Christ's undertaking this Way is what makes possible the Christian's journey in the first place. Christ's Way is ultimately what Augustine understands by grace; a way that is, he teaches, both *sacramentum* (sacrament) and *exemplum* (example). *Sacramentum* was the Latin word for mystery, and meant all that was incomprehensible and unfathomable about God's love for us in Christ. The mystery is that we are saved by the self-emptying Way of the Son of God made flesh. The second term, *exemplum*, is not what we might understand by "example": I give you an example but then the rest is up to you. Christ's example is an "enabling" example. He does indeed show us how to live but in the very "showing" we are enabled to so live — perhaps we could call this showing "exemplary grace" — it is effective and makes our following the Way possible. It is important to insist upon Augustine's understanding of the Way of Christ as being the Son of God's own saving activity on our behalf, his Way, the journey that was his — we don't undertake the journey, we might say, the journey takes us on! This takes the focus away from us and our steps and directs the gaze of our heart towards Christ.

This emphasis on the Way of Christ is profoundly Trinitarian. Christ's Way reveals "the Christo-centric design of God".[3] The Son reveals the Father and promises the Spirit. One of Augustine's favourite scriptural texts is Romans 5:5: "The love of God has been poured forth into our hearts by the Holy Spirit who has been given to us".

> *So it is God the Holy Spirit proceeding from God [the Father] who fires us to the love of God and neighbour when he has been given to us, and he himself is love (Trin. 15.31; see Jo. ev. tr. 39.5).*

> *Anyone with enough mental agility should here follow your apostle, who tells us that "the love of God has been poured forth into our hearts through the Holy Spirit who has been given us". But then, minded to instruct us on spiritual matters, the apostle points out a way of loftiest excellence, the way of love* (viam caritatis); *and*

*he kneels before you on our behalf, entreating
you to grant us some knowledge of the love of
Christ* (scientiam caritatis Christi), *which is exalted above all other knowledge (conf. 13.7.8).*

These comments are Trinitarian through and through.
For Augustine, Rm. 5:5 is one of many texts that speak
of *love* as God's design for humanity — and this love is
God: *Deus caritas est* (see 1 John 4:8 and *Trin.* 15.45).
Christ reveals God's way of love and to come to know
Christ is to come to know God's love, is to come to know
God as Father, Son, and Holy Spirit. The Way of Christ
is ever a Trinitarian Way.

Walk the way of the heart (see s. 4.9)

One of the undeniable features of the Augustinian Way
is its emphasis on the heart: it is a way of interiority.
Interiority is, perhaps, a dangerous word since it is so
easily misunderstood. For many it can connote subjec-
tivism, escapism, individualism, emotionalism — a pri-
vatised religion and spirituality. Nothing could be
further from Augustine's understanding of *heart* — *cor*
or his *way of interiority. Cor*, and perhaps it is helpful
to use the Latin word since it suggests a more "technical" meaning, is above all a biblical word for Augustine.
We have already noted an important text for Augustine,
Romans 5.5, which speaks of God's love poured into our
"*hearts*". It was the heart of Pharaoh that God hardened
(see Rm. 9:17–18) and the hearts of the disciples that
were opened and burned with faith when they were met

by the Risen Jesus on the road to Emmaus (see Lk. 24:32). The psalmist spoke constantly to Augustine about the heart (see, e.g. *en. Pss.* 7.9; 33.1.9; 50.15; 85.7; 134.16; 126; 146.5–6) and it is no wonder that Augustine could exclaim in his *Confessions*:

> *You shattered my heart with your word* (percussisti cor meum verbo tuo) *(conf. 10.6.8).*

> *You pierced our heart with your love, and we bore your piercing words in our depths* (sagittaveras tu cor nostrum caritate tua, et gestabamus verba tua transfixa visceribus . . .) *(ibid., 9.2.3).*

> *My heart is the place where I am whoever I am* (cor meum, ubi ego sum quicumque sum).

This attention to the heart prepares for the way of interiority:

> *Return to your heart* (redi ad cor) *and see there what you may be thinking about God. For there [at your heart] is the image of God. In the interiority of your humanity Christ dwells, there within you are being renewed according to God's image. Recognise its author in the author's image (Jo. ev. tr. 18.10).*

Yet it is not so much the term *cor* that matters most, it is the "interiority" that it represents. For my inner self is my truest self, my authentic self, the self God created and imprinted with the divine image (*imago Dei*, Gen.

1:27). The heart represents and symbolises that God is at the very centre of my own existence and identity. Without God, I am not! To diminish that relationship is, in the final analysis, to diminish myself. The God of my heart (see *conf.* 4.2.3; 9.13.35; *en. Pss.* 36.I.5; 72; 31; *civ. Dei* 10.25) resolves the perennial "either/or" question (God or me), for without the God of my heart I am only "without"! The opposite of the way of the heart is the "way of exteriority". It is to be "outside" of my own self: "You were within, it was I who was outside" (*conf.* 10.27.38)! Thus God is nearer to Augustine than he to himself (ibid., 3.7.12). Accordingly, we must learn to live, so to speak, from the "inside" out.

Augustine's privileged teacher in this regard was St Paul who taught him much about the *homo interior* (2 Cor. 4:16; see Rm. 7:14*ff.*). To live "outside", "exteriorly", means to cling to what is passing and transitory. When Augustine is speaking of "interior/exterior" he is not talking about geography or anatomy! He is talking about identity, being, reality! Thus when he talks about "our restless heart" (*cor nostrum inquietum*) at the outset of his *Confessions* he is talking about our own deepest sense of connectedness with God that will not be satisfied elsewhere. Augustine develops a rich and charged vocabulary to both educate us and awaken us to our own heart, though he offers us no programmed recipe or automatic formula as such for undertaking the journey to our heart. Instead he speaks to us of the need for silence, openness to God's word, an awareness of our body as from God and not substitution for God, a sense of discipline, docility, and above all a desire to have our heart turned toward God: *sursum cor ad Dominum* (see e.g., *ss.* 25.2; 227; 229A.3; *Jo. ev. tr.* 56.5). It is precisely because of this *God-directionality* that Augustinian interiority never becomes closed in upon itself — for the love of God that is the heart's intent is a catholic love, a universal love (see *c. Gaud.* 2.13.14; *ep.* 128.44; *c. litt. Pet.* 3.10.11; *Emer.* 5).

The Lord guides our steps to seek refuge in grace, to want his Way (see correct. 1.2)

Anyone familiar with the name St Augustine ought immediately to think of the word "grace". Within the Western Christian tradition, he is known as the *Doctor of Grace* and there can be no doubt that defending and describing grace prompted some of his most important and even controversial writing and preaching. The Augustinian Way is a way of grace, a way made possible by grace. Perhaps to insist upon the importance of grace for the spirituality of Augustine can seem somewhat speculative and theoretical — academic theology rather than lived spirituality. However, underlying Augustine's uncompromising and unyielding insistence that "all is grace" was a practical conviction and not esoteric argumentation. It was Augustine's profound awareness that to compromise on the question of grace was to compromise our faith in Christ and in the reality of his Incarnation and Redemption (*c. Iul.* 1.6.22).[4] This conviction regarding grace does not come to Augustine in any way other than Scripture — though it was certainly nourished by his own experience of unexpected and unmerited grace. This experience was shaped and clarified by his encounter early on with the writings of Paul, the "Apostle of Grace" (see *gr. et pec. or.* 1.5.6). From the beginning to the end of Paul's writings, Augustine found nothing other than "the grace of Christ through Jesus Christ our Lord" (see Rm. 7:25a, Old Latin) and texts such as "What do you have that you have not received? And if you have received it, why do you boast as if you had not received it" (1 *Cor.* 4:7).

Augustine was acutely aware of how radical and unthinkable was the Son of God's Incarnation. In Jesus Christ humanity and divinity are perfectly united but that union required nothing other than the *humility of God — humilitas Dei —* the *kenosis* of the Son, merited much pondering on Augustine's part. It tells us how desperate was the human situation for the Son to so humbly empty himself. As only God can do, divine grace does not violate us in any way — we were made for God, grace fulfils us, makes us who we were meant to be in the first place — but even goes further, since God now shares human nature in a mysterious and wondrous way. The Augustinian Way, in that sense, is not about heroics, is not about asceticism, is not about spiritual athleticism — we don't save ourselves, *prove* ourselves to God, *make* ourselves worthy of God, *merit* the reward of salvation. Is that meant to discourage us, or to turn us toward passivity or quietism? That certainly was not Augustine's intention. Augustine's own labours are a clear indication that the emphasis on grace is not an excuse for inactivity. Yet the grace question for Augustine is a reminder that the Christian life is not about "programmes" or "spiritual routines" or "ascetical calisthenics", all designed to make us *fit* for God. Grace is really about relationship, our relationship with God as creator and saviour: it is a relationship of divine initiative and merciful love. In the face of that initiative, that grace, we are receptive (in a dynamic and active way), we are grateful, but most especially we are humble!

This Way consists, first, of humility, second, of humility, and third, of humility (ep. 118.22)

The Augustinian Way is a way of humility — it is an integral dimension of Augustine's insistence upon grace. But once again it must be remembered that humility for Augustine is essentially *humilitas Dei*, most especially the Son of God's humility in becoming flesh, and in submitting that flesh to crucifixion.

> *What a humiliation for the Lord, to become a human being! But listen further. He was humbled by becoming man. What more? "He humbled himself", the Apostle says, "becoming obedient even unto death." Not just even unto becoming human but also, "even unto death" (s. 159A.5, Dolbeau 13).*

Humility sums up the human life of Christ for Augustine and this is what makes the way of humility so important for him — humility is the way of Christ. Thus humility is not what *we* do before God but what God

has first done on our behalf. It is the source of our redemption and so our own humility is simply a participation in the humility of Christ. At the moment of his
conversion, when he heard the Pauline call to "put on
Christ" (Rm. 13: 13), Augustine realised that this meant
above all else to put on the humility of Christ, realised
in his total seeking of the Father's will, in his forgiveness of even those who crucified him. It even continues
now in his identification with the poor.

> *Give to your needy brother or sister. To which*
> *one? To Christ. Because anyone who is your*
> *brother or sister is Christ. And because you give*
> *to Christ, you give to God . . . God wanted to be*
> *in need before you, and you withdraw your*
> *hand? (en. Ps. 147.13).*

Humility enables us to realise that we have nothing that
we have not received, and so leads to generosity, compassion, forgiveness and love. Augustinian humility is
not about grovelling, it is about gratitude and generosity. Aware of the giftedness of our life and of our salvation, our heart is opened to the other. We are all God's
beggars, *mendici enim Dei sumus* (*s.* 61.8) Augustine is
fond of saying. This ought not to close our hearts and
turn us into misers, but wonderfully open them into a
spirituality of hospitality that flows from our own gratitude. A noted Augustinian scholar, Tarcisius Van Bavel,
OSA, sums up well the fruits of this kind of humility
upon our own heart: "We can only live together in this
world if we desire all other human beings to live within

our own hearts".[5] The mystery is that Christ's humility
was his exaltation and ours, and the same is true for us
— our humility leads to the lifting up of others. It leads
us to compassionate sharing because we ourselves know
the giftedness that we are. *"Et ipsa bona merita nostra
nonnisi Dei dona esse fateamur* — we confess that even
our good merits are nothing other than God's gifts" (*c.
Iul.* 6.39). Humility opens our heart to love.

Walk in love (ep. 148.1)

Some of the most beautiful mystical love poetry of early
Christianity came from the pen of Augustine:

> *Late have I loved you, o beauty so ancient, so*
> *   new!*
> *Late have I loved you!*
> *For behold you were within me, it was I who was*
> *   not home!*
> *I sought you outside and*
> *In my unloveliness I seized upon those lovely*
> *   things you made.*
> *You were with me, but I was not with you.*
> *Those things kept me far from you which*
> *If they were not in you, would not even be!*
> *You called and cried out and shattered my*
> *   deafness;*
> *Your light burst upon me, flashed before me,*
> *   banished my blindness.*
> *You breathed your fragrance upon me, I drew in*
> *   my breath, and*
> *I now yearn for you.*

> *I tasted, and now I hunger and thirst.*
> *You touched me — and I burned for your peace*
>   *(conf. 10.27.38).*

There is no question that the Augustinian Way is a way of love. This certainly finds its inspiration in Augustine's own restless heart. At the outset of the *Confessions* we discover Augustine the lover as he recounts his arrival in Carthage: "I was in love with loving . . ." (*conf.* 3.1.1). He found within an insatiable hunger for love but the path he chose was anything but true love.

> *Loving and being loved were sweet to me, the more so if I could also enjoy a lover's body; so I polluted the stream of friendship with my filthy desires and clouded its purity with hellish lusts . . . I blundered headlong in the love which I hoped would hold me captive . . . (ibid.).*

This intensity of love explains so much of Augustine.

> *Give me a lover, such a one will know that of which I speak; give me one who longs, who hungers, who is a thirsty pilgrim in the wilderness, sighing for the springs of the eternal homeland; give me such a one, they will know what I mean (Jo. ev. tr. 26.4–5; see s. 131.2.2).*

Indeed Augustine's heart was that of a lover and he finally found the meaning and task of true love, God's love, in the Scriptures. He marvelled at the love of the Beloved Disciple resting his head upon the Lord's bosom: *super pectus domini*. It was a sign not only of remarkable intimacy but of Jesus' willingness and openness to such love. He pondered the bold affirmation of 1 John — *God is love* — and left us with a remarkable commentary on that letter that is a masterpiece of ancient wisdom on the discernment of love. He can thus confidently assert in the *De doctrina Christiana* that everything contained in Scripture is nothing other that an elaboration and explanation of the two-fold love command (see *doc. Chr.* 1.40). Yet Augustine as a critical thinker was well aware of the difficulties, ambiguities and mystery of love. What often passes for love is not love at all:

> *It is better to scold with your mouth and forgive in your heart than to flatter with your mouth and stay cruel in your heart. For thus do undisciplined youth, unwilling to be paddled, plead with us when we wish to discipline: "I sinned, forgive me [Augustine repeats the plea three times!]. And when the paddling begins: "have I offended you up to seventy-seven times?" . . . What is one to do? Let us correct verbally, and when necessary, by paddling . . . (s. 83.8).*

He uses here the example of a young son who quotes the scriptures back to his father (Mt. 18:21–22), but loving discipline must take precedence.

> *If you scold, love inwardly. When you're admonishing, coaxing, correcting, punishing: love and do what you will. A father indeed does not hate his son, yet when it is necessary he must*

> *apply the paddle; pain is inflicted so that health
> may be protected (s. 163B.3).*

> *It is human to get angry — and would that we
> would not be able to — it is human to get angry,
> yet your wrath, like a sudden sprout, must not
> be watered by suspicions and grow into a tree
> trunk of hatred. Anger is one thing, hatred is
> something else. For often a father will get angry
> at his son but he does not hate him. He gets an-
> gry in order to correct him. If for the sake of
> correction someone gets angry, in a loving way
> he is getting angry (s. 211.1).*

It is precisely for this reason that Augustine devoted much attention to an ordered love, *ordo amoris* (see *civ. Dei* 15.22; *ench.* 20.45; *b. conjug.* 3.3.). Our task is to order our loves (e.g., *ep.* 140.2), a Scriptural charge he discovered in the course of his pondering the *Canticle of Canticles* (2.4): "order love within me — *ordinate in me caritatem.*" It took one well-known and controversial form in his distinction between "*frui*" and "*uti*". The first Latin word means literally to "*enjoy*", the second to "*use*". Regarding love, Augustine says we can "enjoy God" (*frui*) alone. Everything other than God must be "used" (*uti*). The modern reader might respond immediately that this sounds more like "abuse" than "love", but one must read Augustine carefully and widely to appreciate what exactly he meant. In the highly oral–rhetorical society that was his, emphasis often took the form of provocative statements. Taken at face value, one could take statements too exclusively, too literally. Both *frui* and *uti* are, in that sense, technical words. What Augustine is insisting upon, really, is an ordering of our loves. Only God can be treated as the subject of our ultimate love — all other loves must be distinguished from this absolute love because all other loves are created, limited, imperfect, vulnerable. We ourselves are, one might say, guilty of "idolatry" or "abuse" by loving anyone or anything in the same way we love God. Thus "*uti*" does not mean "not to love"; it doesn't mean we take advantage of people or use them as disposable items for our own benefit, rather it means that we love according to God's order.

The King of the city has made himself the Way for us to reach his city (see en. Ps. 86.1).

One key direction that this ordering of love took was that of community — and community, for Augustine, takes many forms: church, family, friendship, monastery, the poor, the city, civil society. Augustine even acknowledges the existence of "anti-communities" such as a band of robbers. We begin life, he notes, "in community":

> It is to see our parents that we first open our
> eyes, and this life [of ours] takes its beginning
> from their friendship (ad parentes enim suos
> homo aperit oculos, et haec vita ab eorum
> amicitia sumit exordium) *(s. 9.7).*

These comments are echoed in Augustine's opening remarks in his *De bono coniugali* (I.1) regarding the importance of the friendship of husband and wife and the unity of their love as the foundation of the marriage commitment: "the first natural bond of human society is that of husband and wife". There is a pervasive attention to community throughout Augustine's writings, one that finds its greatest realisation in his explorations of the community that is the church.

> *Shared was our loss, shared be our finding* (communis fuit perditio, sit communis inventio) *(s. 115.4.4).*

Church for Augustine was not a question of sectarianism (though some will read him this way!), nor was it a question of convenience (it was anything but convenient, for it demanded forbearance and forgiveness), nor was it a substitute for personal holiness and responsibility (his ecclesiology never allowed for the group to supply for individual conversion). It was the way God had chosen: *salus extra ecclesiam non est* (*bapt.* 4.17.24). However, the church is never simply "church", for it is always understood to be the *ecclesia Christi* — the *church of Christ*, God's church (see e.g. *s.* 346B.3). The scriptures and the sacraments are unthinkable without the church and the church is unthinkable without the scriptures and the sacraments; it is the economy of salvation chosen by God (see *c. Jul.* I.30). At a time when memory of persecution was still fresh, when many were still "outside the church" and thus "outside of Christ", pastors, spiritual guides, and theologians like Augustine were in no position to even imagine themselves speculating about "anonymous Christians" —

though Augustine will tantalising and discreetly hint at
the mysterious and saving ways of God that extend beyond the visible boundaries of the Church (see *s.*
198.32, *Dolbeau* 26). However, Augustine has no doubt
that *the* community of salvation is the church, richly
described in the *Book of Acts* and serving as model for
all future expressions of church. This first church (see
doct. chr. 3.6) offers the model for what a true community of love should be.

Augustine loved to explore the description of the
first Christian community in Jerusalem contained in
the *Book of Acts*. In it he found clearly stated the profile
and values for every and all Christian communities,
communities formed by resurrection faith. He was particularly taken by Acts 4:31–35 with its portrayal of the
apostolic community as being "one soul and one heart
(*anima una et cor unum*)" (Acts 4:32) and allowing for
no one to be in need. This account offered both identity
and task for every Christian community in all its manifestations: from church gathered around Eucharistic
altar to family gathered around dinner table, to monastic community gathered around God in a shared commitment (*propositum*). In fact, he found in this
narrative one of the most important summations of
what the little monastic community he gathered around
him was to be: *anima una et cor unum*. Yet so that neither he nor anyone else would perhaps be tempted to
turn this into simply safe haven or exclusive social club
he added to the Latin expression the words "*in Deum*":
"one soul and one heart on the way to God (*anima una*

et cor unum in Deum)". Not only was he willing to "amend" the Scriptures, certainly by way of clarification, but to do so in a succinct but telling way. *In Deum* are words for someone "on the way", the Latin demanding a dynamic translation: "on the way to God", "towards God", "into God". This is how Augustine wanted to live a community of love and, on one occasion, having read the text from Acts, he did something out of the ordinary to make just this point:

> *I too want to read it. It gives me more pleasure, you see, to be reading these words than to be arguing my case with my own words [he repeats the text just read from Acts] . . . You have heard what our wishes are; pray that we may be able to live up to them (s. 356.1–2).*

The Augustinian Way is a way of love and for this reason the journey is never a solitary one. The way is traversed by a journeying pilgrim community of love.

> *Let us ascend, let us sing, let us make progress — so that we may arrive (adscendamus, cantemus, et proficiamus, ut perveniamus) (en. Ps. 125.15).*

I will give you understanding and set you upon the Way by which you will enter (Trin 3.19)

Perhaps by now it is clear that the Augustinian Way is quite straightforward — it is simply the way of Christ. But if the Way is simple, Augustine insists we are not! God indeed is One and so not "confused" nor "change-

able" (*civ. Dei.* 11.10) — but such is not our situation as
creatures! Beyond our fragile creaturely status and a
direct consequence of the Fall, Augustine will insist, is
our present *ignorantia* — ignorance. We do not know,
nor are we necessarily good learners or thinkers: we err,
we misread, we misunderstand, we fail to grasp the
truth. Yet, for Augustine, it is in our minds, in our intelligence, that we are made to the image and likeness of
God. Grace thus not only purifies us from sin but also
opens us to understanding: "pray for understanding" he
insists (*orate ut intelligatis, gr. et lib. arb.* 46). In that
sense it can be said that the Augustinian Way is one
where learning, thinking, understanding, reading and
study, dialectics and dialogue are viewed as potential
spiritual practices to help us make our way. Augustine
took his Septuagint translation of Isaiah 7:9, "Unless
you believe, you will not understand", as a God-given
warrant to incorporate the intellectual life into the spiritual life. In Mt. 7:7 Jesus teaches us to ask, seek, knock
— Augustine read these words as inviting all Christians
into Christ's school where together we can learn the
Way as fellow-students before the podium of the One
Master, the One Teacher. Augustine was well aware of
the constant temptation of the "learned" to succumb to
pride but this was no excuse for not learning — rather it
was a reminder to learn humbly (see *ep.* 186.7). The
Augustinian Way is a way of learning, of study, of in-
quiry — so that God's Truth may ever more completely
be our guide.

Conclusion

> *Accept the sacrifice of my confessions, offered to*
> *you by the power of this tongue of mine which*
> *you have fashioned and aroused to confess to*
> *your name . . . (conf. 5.1.1).*

So much of the Augustinian Way is summed up as well
as modelled in Augustine's perhaps most famous of his
works, the *Confessions*. This remarkably original work
not only recounts Augustine's journey, it stands equally
as an invitation for anyone who would take it up to
awaken to the call of their own journey.

> *So, then, when I confess not what I have been*
> *but what I am now, this is the fruit to be reaped*
> *from my confessions: I confess not only before*
> *you in secret exultation tinged with fear and se-*
> *cret sorrow infused with hope, but also in the*
> *ears of believing men and women, the compan-*
> *ions of my joy and sharers in my mortality, my*
> *fellow citizens still on pilgrimage with me, those*
> *who have gone before and those who will fol-*
> *low, and all who bear me company in my life*
> *(10.4.6).*

The Augustinian Way will always remain a way of *con-*
fessio, this Latin term being much richer than its English equivalent since it first means to praise God and
only then to acknowledge one's sins. Those who would
wish to learn more of this way could do no better than
to prayerfully and reflectively take up his *Confessions*
and let the One Teacher do the rest:

If you want to be led by the way of faith to the possession of the vision, begin with confession (en. Ps. 146.14).

Notes

[1]   For citations of Augustine's works I am following the abbreviations used in Allan Fitzgerald, OSA (General Editor) (1999), *Augustine through the Ages: An Encyclopedia*, Grand Rapids, MI: William B. Eerdmans Publishing Company.

[2]   The English text of the *Confessions* is based upon Maria Boulding, OSB's (1997) translation in the series *The Works of Saint Augustine: A Translation for the 21st Century*, editor, John E. Rotelle, OSA, New York: New City Press.

[3]   See the comments by Pierre-Marie Hombert (1996), *Gloria Gratiae: Se glorifier en Dieu, principe et fin de la théologie augustinienne de la grace*, Paris: Institut d'Études Augustiniennes, p. 575.

[4]   Hombert, 255.

[5]   T.J. Van Bavel (1980), *Christians in the World: Introduction to the Spirituality of St Augustine*, New York: Catholic Book Publishing Co., p. 41.

2

BENEDICTINE SPIRITUALITY

Andrew Nugent, OSB

Benedictine Life: The Slow-Release Miracle

It is said that the *Rule of St Benedict* has been translated more often than any other book except the Bible.[1] There are at least a dozen English versions currently in circulation, and scores of others in many languages. The secondary literature, too, is enormous, ranging from commentaries, through monographs on literary, historical, and spiritual aspects of the *Rule*, to books, articles, tapes, and CDs presenting monastic life in a great variety of different perspectives: popular piety, therapy, alternative lifestyle, neo-romanticism, gnosticism for the elite, basic Christianity for everyone, school of prayer, mystic path — the list is extensive. There is also a considerable and growing documentation on Benedictine and Cistercian art, architecture, and music, on monastic liturgy and prayer. Most monasteries have their own literature. Many, ancient or modern, extinct or extant, are still attracting enthusiastic pilgrims and sight-seers. Finally,

and increasingly, there are comparative studies about
Eastern and Western, Christian and non-Christian forms
of monasticism, and specifically about the possibility and
problems of implanting Benedictine and Cistercian life in
non-European cultures.

Significant contributions are being made in this
whole area by people who are neither monks nor nuns
nor, in some cases, Christians or believers. Culturally,
their interest is understandable because monasticism
did play an important role in the emergence of contemporary Western civilisation. What is less obvious is why
so many people, scholars and simple folk alike, still find
Benedict's wisdom and way of life relevant and enrich-
ing, in an era when so much else that seemed valuable
and good has been left behind.

Benedict would be the first to express surprise, were
he to return today, 1,500 years after his death. He
would be astonished to learn that he had founded a
great religious order which has lasted until the present
time, and even more astounded to hear that he is regarded as the *Patron of Europe*, albeit in ever increasing and distinguished company. He would probably
need explanations about what a religious order is and
parameters to the political and social concept of
Europe. Not much of all that has happened over the
centuries in his name would seem to have featured on
Benedict's original agenda. He did not plan things that
way. His simple life sowed a seed: God gave the growth
and the harvest.

This seems characteristic of Benedictine life even today. Its essential witness and apostolate are no more specific or proactive than the overriding principle that Benedict took from Scripture and enshrined in his *Rule*: *that in all things God may be glorified.*[2] The emphasis is not on what a person or a community can achieve for the Church and society, but on whether they are striving for that *purity of heart* in God's service without which all achievement is ultimately self-serving.[3]

Benedict was born about 480 AD at Nursia, northeast of Rome, and never strayed more than a few days' journey from the place of his birth. He was moderately well educated up to the age of 16 or 17, when he fled, *scienter indoctus,*[4] from the worldly or worse atmosphere of student life in Rome. Settling in a cave in the hill country of Subiaco, he lived as a hermit until early manhood. Then, coaxed from his solitude by some neighbouring monks who thought he might make a good abbot, he eventually founded twelve monasteries.

If two attempts on his life are anything to go by, Benedict was hardly a great abbot at that time. Too ardent perhaps, too idealistic; he was certainly inexperienced and probably intolerant. His famous *Rule for Monks*, written some 40 years later at Monte Cassino, bears all the signs of holy wisdom, gentle patience, and a loving understanding of human nature, acquired the hard way, by experience, through many trials, and with not a few mistakes along the way.

Virtually everything we know about Benedict is contained in that *Rule* or in the charming Life of the Saint, written by Pope St Gregory the Great 50 years after his death in 547. There are no spectacular achievements recorded in either document, unless it be some nicely appropriate miracles, which historians would probably discount, or that least dramatic of miracles, which they might not even notice: tiny communities of stable, harmonious, orderly, hospitable, and God-centred life sprouting amidst the rubble of a ransacked and ruined empire.

If men and women today are still turning to communities where *Peace, Work and Pray,* and *Prefer nothing to Christ*, are the familiar watchwords, it is surely not in search of sophisticated ideas or esoteric wisdom. They are attracted by a simple art of spiritual living and by the slow-release miracle of God's fidelity and love in the long endurance of daily life.

Searching for God

A priest coming to join Benedict's monastery was greeted with the words, *Friend, why have you come?* (60:3). Is it coincidence that this is what Jesus said to Judas, who had just arrived to betray him with a kiss? (Matt. 26:50).

Benedictine novices are encouraged to ask themselves frequently, not just during their novitiate but throughout their monastic life, *Why did I come here?* There is a danger that they might forget. The first degree of humility, Benedict tells us, is *to keep the fear of God always before one's eyes, and to shun all forget-fulness* (7:10).

People come to monasteries for all sorts of reasons. Sometimes these reasons are patently inappropriate: to evade conscription into the army or detection by the police, to avoid starvation, to escape domestic unhappiness or professional or moral failure, to flee emotionally or psychologically unmanageable situations. Some people join monasteries to get away from other people, maybe parents or persons of the opposite sex, or just as many people as possible. Others want security, predictability, safe routines, regular feeding, health care and accommodation, without too much bother.

There are also ambivalent motivations. An interest in liturgy, in sacred music, art, scholarship, or some apostolate or activity associated with the particular monastery chosen. One may come, attracted by a charismatic abbot or some other figure within the community whom one perceives as a viable guru or *anam cara*.

Most monastic vocations are buttressed by one or several secondary motivations, some of them quite superficial. The Holy Spirit can use these fads and favourites like booster-rockets to get a neophyte *into orbit*, but none of them has sufficient impetus for the journey still out ahead. Sooner or later, all must burn out and fall away. The vital question then is, what, if anything, is left?

St Benedict is credited with the invention of novitiates and novice-masters, at least in the sense of specifi-

cally designated persons and places, and a prescribed
programme of 12 months' duration. The novitiate was a
time of formation and acclimatisation to the strange
world of monastic living. More essentially, in Benedict's
mind, it was a process of testing and investigation. This
had nothing to do with those regimes of eccentric com-
mands, artificial humiliations, and false accusations
which became fashionable in later, more rococo times.
Quite to the contrary: the essential business of Benedict's novitiate was always, and should still be, reality
and truth.

> *A senior chosen for his skill in winning souls
> should be appointed to look after (the novices)
> with careful attention. His concern must be to
> find out whether the novice truly seeks God
> (58:6).*

There is only *one* necessary and sufficient reason to be
or stay in a monastery: that is the conviction that this is
where God wants me to be, to seek and to find him.
Whether or not *I* want it, in the sense of finding life easy
and the company congenial, is not the essential issue.
Besides, as in marriage and in all walks of life, there are
good times and bad times. The monk must be *ambidex-
trous*, as Cassian says, able to turn bad times and good
to spiritual advantage.[5] His fundamental sense of vocation must be sufficiently deep and focused to survive
both. Monasteries are not spiritual comfort-zones. They
are *schools of the Lord's service* (Prol. 45).

Fundamental Perspectives

Reverential awe, it has been said, *is the central spiritual value of Benedict's Rule.*[6] The monastery is the household of God in whose presence the monk is living at every moment and wherever he may be:

> *at the work of God, in the oratory, in the monastery, in the garden, on the road, in a field, or anywhere else, whether he is sitting, walking or standing (7:63).*

It is this fundamental reality of God's presence which inspires and motivates the profound sentiments of attentiveness, obedience, humility, reverence and love which should characterise every aspect of monastic life.

Reverential awe is not servile fear. On the contrary, Benedict promises that, by the Holy Spirit's action, all that we initially perform with dread, we will *soon* begin to observe through:

> *the perfect love of God which casts out fear (1 Jn 4:18), without effort, as though naturally, from habit, no longer out of fear of hell, but out of love for Christ, good habit, and delight in virtue (7:67–70).*

Three times Benedict tells us that we should *prefer nothing to the love of Christ* (4:21, 5:2, 72:11). Christ is the true king for whom we fight (Prol. 3), whom we follow in hardship (Prol. 50, 4:10) and to glory (Prol. 7). It is Christ that we reverence and serve in our superiors and communities, in guests, the poor, pilgrims and, *above and before all else,* in the sick who must be *truly served as Christ, for he said "I was sick and you visited me" and "what you did for one of these least brothers you did for me"* (36:1–3). To Christ also we turn in times of temptation, dashing our evil thoughts against *the rock which is Christ* (Prol. 28; 4:50).

If we seek God and serve Christ in all these ways, it is because it is He who seeks us first.

> *Seeking His workman in a multitude of people, the Lord calls out, "Is there anyone here who yearns for life and desires to see good days?" If you hear this and your answer is "I do", God then directs these words to you, "If you desire true and eternal life, keep your tongue free from vicious talk and your lips from all deceit; turn away from evil and do good; seek peace and pursue it. Once you have done this, my eyes will be upon you and my ears will listen for your prayers; and even before you ask me, I will say to you: Here I am." What, dear brothers, is more delightful than this voice of the Lord calling to us? See how the Lord in His love shows us the way of life. Clothed then with faith and the performance of good works, let us set out on this way, with the Gospel for our guide, that we may deserve to see Him who has called us to His kingdom (Prol. 14–21).*

The Ladder of Humility

Benedict wishes his disciples' lives and actions to be founded on the truth of the relationship between God and ourselves. Humility is the truthful expression of that relationship. The word *humilitas* comes from *humus*, the good earth. The humble person has his feet on the ground. He lives with reality, the reality of God's utter love as the source of everything that is good, and the truth also of our own sinfulness.

> *Place your hope in God alone. If you notice something good in yourself, give credit to God, not to yourself, but be certain that the evil you commit is always your own and yours to acknowledge (4:41–43).*

Chapter 7 of the *Rule* describes the *ladder of humility* which the monk must climb in order to become grounded in truth and so find God. This ladder has twelve rungs.

1. To fear God.

2. Not to love one's own will.

3. To obey one's superior, *for the love of God.*

4. To endure hard and even unjust treatment with courage and patience.

5. To acknowledge one's own faults.

6. To be content with shabby, even menial conditions, and not to feel that we deserve better.

7. To thank God that our self-importance and pride have been deflated.

8. To follow the example of our elders rather than our own self-will.

9. To measure our words.

10. Not to be shallow and facetious.

11. To be gentle, serious, modest and reasonable in our words.

12. And in our whole demeanour.

These are unusual prescriptions in a culture where self-esteem and personal promotion are greatly prized. Where, we wonder, could such a programme leave us *vis-à-vis* confreres who might take it less seriously than ourselves? Turning the other cheek is only easy when everybody else is doing it as well. And sometimes monasteries are not like that.

But the *ladder of humility* is less about how to live with each other than about how to live together *in the presence of God*. To the extent that we remember this context the steps of humility begin to make sense. To the extent that we exclude God from our tunnel-vision view of human relations, we remain prey to anger, envy, pride, and a whole range of vengeful and malicious thoughts about those around us.

What the *ladder of humility* does is to confront us with the real object of our anger and resentment: God himself. There is an old monastic joke — such things do exist — which goes as follows: *Question:* Why does St Benedict say that the abbot takes the place of Christ in the monastery? *Answer:* Because he is the one that we crucify. Abbots do have a hard time. Monks, like the rest of us, tend to vent their frustrations and insecurities on each other, but especially on their abbots. In Freudian terms, we could see this as a case of Oedipal conflict. An abbot, as the very name suggests, is a *father figure* and as likely a focus for resentment as for reverence.

Freud argues from love and hatred for the *real* father to *religion*, as an obsessive neurosis centred on the mental *projection* we call God. Benedict understands things exactly the other way around. We vent our anger with God and his will on other people, and especially on those who represent his authority. This conflict goes to the heart of the spiritual life, and abbots get crucified in the process.

It is in this context that we can understand Benedict's repeated and severe condemnations of what he calls *murmuring*. This has nothing to do with dislike for complaints or criticism. He is perfectly open to both, expressed in the right way and at the right time. Murmuring, in Benedict's view, is a quite different exercise — underhand, corrosive, and highly dangerous in community because it undermines the faith/trust relationship between the brethren and God himself. Murmuring is cowardly, not so much because it is done behind people's backs, which it nearly always is, but because we

make other people whipping boys for our own failures
in obedience and trust.[7]

Christ had no complaints about his judges and exe-
cutioners. They are to be forgiven because *they do not
know what they are doing* (Lk. 23:34). But what exactly did he mean when he told Pilate, *You would have
no power over me if it had not been given you from
above; that is why the one who handed me over to you
has the greater responsibility* (Jn. 19:11)? Is he merely
blaming Judas and the Jewish authorities? And when
he cried out on the cross, *My God, my God, why have
you deserted me?* (Mt. 27:46), is he simply reciting his
psalter? We know that from the outset, quite apart from
the grubby political and financial calculations of Judas
and Caiaphas, there is a potential clash of wills between
Jesus and the Father about his fate, a clash which can
only be resolved by *kenosis,* self-emptying, the free and
loving submission of the Son to his Father's will (Mt.
26:39ff).

St Benedict defines monastic life in terms of this
Paschal experience of Christ.

> *Persevering in his teaching in the monastery
> until death, we shall share by patience in the
> sufferings of Christ that we may deserve to
> share also in his kingdom (Prol. 50).*

The *ladder of humility* helps us to recognise the real
issues in our spiritual life, how much anger, pride, and
resentment smoulder in our hearts, how pitiless and
unloving we can be with those around us, but, behind

all that and largely unacknowledged, how little we trust God and how ill-disposed we are to accept his will, which is always the expression of his boundless love.

The steps of humility are not a checklist of unpleasant things we have to do to ourselves in order to arrive at some notional perfection. They are, rather, a phenomenology of God's creative action within us. Benedict is describing how grace transforms us into people who, accepting ever more willingly what God is doing in our lives, become progressively more aware of who we really are. This self-knowledge is the basis of true peace and personal integration. It is a wonderful grace to be able to watch, *and assent to*, the miracle of our own creation.

> *All this the Lord will by the Holy Spirit graciously show forth* (demonstrare) *in his workman now cleansed of vices and sins (7:70).*

We have in this *demonstration* of the Holy Spirit not only a mirror for the purest form of self-love, but also the foundation for a theology of monastic witness. This will never be a matter of putting on a show of superiority or holiness. Nothing could be more obnoxious than that, and Benedict warns us against it (4:62). But a monastic community, and each member of it, can be and should be a *monstrance* for the ongoing slow-release miracle of God's creative love.

The flowering of that love comes in the utter humility of death. In contrast to when we were first born, we can now freely assent to God's gift of new life.

Signs of the Seeker

We have anticipated the happy ending. We must now go back to the beginning.

Having asked the Novice-Master to investigate whether the novice *truly seeks God,* Benedict goes on to explain what areas need scrutiny in order to arrive at a reliable answer to that question: *Is he zealous for the Work of God, for obedience, and for trials?* Clearly believing that each of these facets of monastic life is going to be difficult and to test the candidate's mettle, he adds with characteristic forthrightness that *the novice should be clearly told all the hardships and difficulties through which we journey to God* (58:7–8), so that he or she will fully realise *what they are getting into* (58:12).

Zealous for the Work of God

What does it mean? In pre-Benedictine monastic tradition, the expression *work of God* (*opus Dei*) meant anything and everything done in God's service. Benedict, who uses the expression 16 times, gives it a much sharper focus: the *work of God* means the community prayer of the monastic family. What is required is a faithful commitment to the worship of God within and together with the worshipping community of God's household (the *domus Dei*). For monks and nuns, this will be their monastic community. For lay people, if the opportunity offers, it may be an association with a community, a less formalised group, their own family, or their parish church.

The monks of Egypt laid more stress on continuous personal prayer than on communal worship. Benedict's few years as a teenage hermit living in his cave seem to reach back to that venerable tradition. His biographer, Pope St Gregory the Great, depicts, with surprising equanimity, a life in which community worship, sacramental piety, and even ecclesial adherence played little if any part. It is indeed remarkable that a saint popularly believed to have founded an order of dedicated liturgists could have gone so "low church" at one point as not even to know when it was Easter Sunday. Even today, non-practice does not come any worse than that.[8]

This a-liturgical Benedict might appeal to the spiritual cave-dwellers of our own day, those who *truly seek God*, but are not attracted, or may even be repelled by the facts and fictions of Church life or by the often distorted perceptions of the churches in our increasingly dysfunctional cultures. Pope Gregory says, in praise of Benedict the cave-dweller, that *he dwelt with himself.* He goes on to explain what that means:

> *Every time we are led outside ourselves by excessive concern, we remain ourselves but we are no longer with ourselves because, having lost sight of ourselves, we wander in alien places.*

Although in later years Benedict discouraged others tempted to emulate his youthful eremitical enthusiasm (1:3–5), it is precisely in the ex-centricity and inchoateness of his pristine ardour that young people today, ambivalent about commitment and belonging, may find him attractive and strangely contemporary. Not many are likely to go and live in caves. They may nonetheless need their own experience, just as he did.

The mature Benedict of the *Rule* says categorically: *Let nothing be put before the Work of God* (43:3). This is in no way a plea for the sort of ornate and elaborate liturgy sometimes associated with Benedictines in later centuries. Neither does it mean that he had any explicit sense of the monastic liturgy as the "official prayer of the Church". It is nevertheless a firm assertion of the central importance of community worship in Christian life. This intuition remains as perhaps the most significant witness of monks to the Church and to the world.

> *We believe that the divine presence is every-where and that "in every place the eyes of the Lord are watching the good and the wicked" (Prov. 15:3). But beyond the least doubt we should believe this to be especially true when we celebrate the Divine Office.*

> *We must always remember, therefore, what the Prophet says: "Serve the Lord with fear" (Ps. 2:11), and again, "Sing praise wisely" (Ps. 47:8); and, "In the presence of the angels I will sing to you" (Ps 138:1). Let us consider, then, how we ought to behave in the presence of God and his angels, and let us stand to sing the psalms in such a way that our minds are in har-mony with our voices (19 passim).*

This spirit of reverence permeates Benedict's attitude to every aspect of the liturgy. So it is that, at the singing of the doxology, all *rise from their seats in honour and reverence for the Holy Trinity* (9:7), and *stand with respect and awe* when the Gospel is proclaimed (11:9). Some people feel that the size and fervour of Sunday congregations might increase if there were more emphasis on reverence and less on human inventiveness. The two are surely not incompatible.

Towards the end of his life, Benedict had a vision in which he saw the whole of creation as if contained in a ball of light. He understood how God's presence and love are everywhere. So, too, our love and worship should encounter God's goodness everywhere. This is the secret of the profound respect for each person that Benedict constantly urges, but also for his insistence that even the humblest *things* should be treated with reverence. So the monk must *look upon all the utensils and goods of the monastery as sacred vessels of the altar, aware that nothing should be neglected* (31:10), and *whoever fails to keep the things belonging to the monastery clean or treats them carelessly should be reproved* (32:4). This is also why monks must:

> *look to the father of the monastery for all their needs. . . . All things should be the common possession of all, as it is written (Acts 4:32), so that no one presumes to call anything his own (33:5–6).*

We are not individual owners, but brothers and sisters who jointly steward and share the wonders of God's creation. These intuitions are richer and more meaningful than ever today, at a time when concern for the environment and for our common birthright has reached global dimensions. Today, *preferring nothing to the work of God* means circling the entire planet with our shared reverence and worship.

First-time readers of Benedict's *Rule* are disappointed to find so little about personal prayer and nothing at all about contemplation or mysticism. There is no mention of stages or degrees of prayer, no techniques are suggested for meditation, nor is there any advice about how to cope with dryness or distractions. Benedict is at the furthest remove from envisaging prayer as a neo-gnostic delight for initiates or a well-crafted aesthetically pleasing experience for spiritual gourmets.

Benedict is very sensitive to the differences between people and how uniquely the Spirit acts in each individual soul. If he hesitates to legislate for other people's eating and drinking (40:1–2), how much more reticent will he be about quantifying or measuring their personal prayer. Chapter 20, "On reverence in prayer", is a model of this discretion. Benedict recommends *humility and pure devotion*. He continues:

> *Let us realise that we shall be heard not in much speaking, but in purity of heart and in compunction and tears.*

His conclusion is equally forthright:

> *and that is why prayer should be brief and*
> *pure, unless it be prolonged by an inspiration of*
> *divine grace.*

Benedict repeats frequently throughout the *Rule* his advice that prayer should be simple and heartfelt.

> *If at other times he wishes to pray more secretly*
> *by himself, let him simply go in to the oratory*
> *and pray, not with a loud voice but with tears*
> *and an attentive heart (52:4).*

Prayer with tears is a recurring theme (4:57; 49:4). The emphasis is never on methods or techniques, but always on sincerity, attentiveness, spontaneity, and quality rather than quantity.[9]

We have to read what Benedict says about prayer against the background of a whole monastic spirituality which he inherited from the Fathers and Mothers of the Desert. Two fundamental themes in that spirituality are *purity of heart* and *lectio Divina.*

Purity of Heart

The immediate goal of monastic life is to achieve, through asceticism and in combat against evil thoughts, *purity of heart.* This means progressively freeing oneself, by God's grace, from the tyranny of the *logismoi,* those evil thoughts which alienate us from God, from our true selves, and from reality. To the extent that the monk advances in this healing process, he lives more and more permanently in God's presence and with the truth about himself and about the whole of creation. This is, in effect, to live in continuous prayer. Benedict's *Rule* is a phenomenology of this growth in interior life. It is how he teaches prayer, and it is worth a thousand manuals.[10]

Lectio Divina

Benedict's monks spent up to three hours a day in the slow prayerful reading of Scripture.

> *Reading, meditation, prayer, contemplation. This is the ladder of monks by which they are lifted up from earth to heaven.*[11]

This reading in depth is "a means of descending to the level of the heart and of finding God".[12] It is the traditional and peculiarly monastic form of prayer.

Zealous for Obedience

Monastic life is not servitude: it is the willing service of free people. The monastery is not a penitentiary: it is the *domus Dei*, the house of God, and the inhabitants are God's household. Accordingly, Benedict always looks beyond mere compliance with rules and regulations to the inner dispositions of the heart.

Hearing that Martin the Hermit had chained himself to a rock in his cave so that he could no longer change his mind about monastic life, Benedict sent him an urgent message that the love of Christ alone should bind us rather than iron chains.[13]

Paradoxically, it is very often the spiritual *cave-dwellers,* who stay away from churches, who also understand intuitively that, behind the façade of routine and ritual, there persists in monastic communities a vibrant freedom which expresses itself *within* the disciplines of worship, asceticism, the common life, work, and hospitality.

The Latin word *oboedire*, to obey, is cognate to the word *obaudire*, to listen. The first word of Benedict's *Rule* is *Listen!* The monk is, or should be, a *listener*. Attentive to the signs of the times, he listens for the word of God in the Scriptures, in the voice of his abbot, in the tradition and teaching of the Church and of the Fathers, in the words and needs of his confreres, and of all with whom he comes in contact, especially the poor and the sick.

The monastic tradition has always recognised self-will as the major obstacle, not only to good community relationships, but to friendship with God himself. It is clear, therefore, how the notions of humility and obedience are virtually interchangeable. Neither has anything whatsoever to do with servility or abjectness. Both require a good sense of oneself and an openness to real relationships.

Ch. 72., "On the Good Zeal which monks should have", is a beautiful summary of St Benedict's wise teaching on obedience:

*Just as there is a wicked zeal of bitterness which
separates from God and leads to hell, so there is
a good zeal which separates from evil and leads
to God and everlasting life. This, then, is the
good zeal which monks must foster with fervent
love: "They should each try to be the first to
show respect to the other" (Rm. 12:10), support-
ing with the greatest patience one another's
weaknesses of body or behaviour, and earnestly
competing in obedience to one another. No one
is to pursue what he judges better for himself,
but instead what he judges better for someone
else. To their fellow monks they show the pure
love of brothers; to God loving fear; to their abbot sincere and humble love. Let them prefer
nothing whatever to Christ, and may he bring
us all together to everlasting life.*

Benedict's abbot is given very wide authority in the
Rule, authority so wide that Canon Law and the Constitutions of the various Benedictine congregations have
seen fit to curtail it, notably in financial matters. But if
the abbot's powers are extensive, they come with prodi-
gal warnings. Several times he is reminded that he will
answer to God for every one of his decisions, that he
must always act with justice, and indeed set mercy
above justice. He must seek:

*profit for the monks, not pre-eminence for him-
self, and strive to be loved rather than feared.
He must be discerning and moderate, bearing
in mind the discretion of holy Jacob, who said,*

> *"If I drive my flocks too hard, they will all die in a single day" (Gen. 33:13). Therefore, drawing on this and other examples of discretion, the mother of virtues, he must so arrange everything that the strong have something to yearn for and the weak nothing to run away from (64: passim).*

Benedict lays down that whenever anything important is to be done in the monastery, the whole community is to be called together, fully briefed on the issues, and asked for their advice. He particularly stresses that *everybody* should be called to counsel. *The reason why we have said all should be called for counsel is that the Lord often reveals what is better to the younger* (3:3). Even in lesser matters, the abbot should seek advice. Benedict quotes the Book of Wisdom: *Do everything with counsel and you will not be sorry afterwards* (*Sir* 32:24).

The abbot is also told all the things he must not be: *Excitable, anxious, extreme, obstinate, jealous or over-suspicious* — and he adds the excellent reason: *Such a man is never at rest* (64:16).

From these remarks, it should be evident that, if the abbot is the most powerful person in the monastery, he must also be the most obedient and the one who listens most. Benedict spells it out:

> *He must know what a difficult and demanding burden he has undertaken: directing souls and serving a variety of temperaments, coaxing*

some, reproving others, encouraging others
again. He must so accommodate and adapt
himself to each one's character and intelligence
that he will not only suffer no loss in the flock
entrusted to his care, but rejoice in the increase
of a good flock (2:3–32).

Zealous for Trials

The word used is *opprobria*. This could mean insults or
contemptuous treatment. Such things can happen in
monasteries as elsewhere, but they are not inherent to
the monastic way of life. Benedict seems to be talking
more about the humble and unpleasant tasks that need
to be done in any household, such as were usually left to
slaves in the ancient world. More generally, he has in
mind how a person reacts in situations where his pride
or his sense of his own dignity, precedence, or compe-
tence is punctured or ignored. One does tend to show
one's true colours when the bubble of conceit is pricked
in these revealing little episodes. Not the least telling
aspect of such apparent trivialities is the extent to
which they can irk and upset us. Benedict, heir to the
wisdom of the desert, has a keen eye for the pettiness
which says, embarrassingly loudly, what we are really
seeking in life.

If we seem to end on an anti-climax, this too is in fidelity to the spirit of Benedict.

Monastic spirituality is for ordinary people with
boring lives. It will disappoint those in search of beautiful and intriguing experiences. The Exodus from Egypt

to the Promised Land leads across the wilderness. The desert is monotonous and the haunt of demons. But it also symbolises in its utter vastness *the infinity of God's love* (Evagrius).

Notes

[1] In the following pages, numbers in brackets refer to chapter and verse in the *Rule of St. Benedict*. The translation generally used is (1980), *RB 80*, Collegeville: Liturgical Press.

[2] 1 Pe 4:11, quoted in *RB* 57:9.

[3] The *immediate* goal of monastic life is to arrive at *purity of heart*, a state of integrity and truth in which everything is attuned to God and no longer distorted by prejudice or passion. See Cassian, *Conf.* 1, and Luckman, H. and Kulzer, L. (eds.) (1999), *Purity of Heart in Early Ascetic and Monastic Literature,* Collegeville: Liturgical Press.

[4] *Wisely unlearned.* Gregory the Great, *Dial.* 2: Prol. Gregory's life of Benedict is contained in Book 2 of his *Dialogues* (with two small additions in later books). See text and commentary by de Vogüé, A. Trans. Costello. H. and de Bhaldraithe, E. (1993), *The Life of St Benedict*, Petersham: St Bede's Publications.

[5] Cassian, *Conf.* 6.

[6] Kardong, T. (1993), "Benedictine Spirituality" in *New Dictionary of Catholic Spirituality*, Collegeville: Liturgical Press, pp. 84–91.

[7] See Nugent, A. (1995) "Towards a Pathology of Community Life" in *Religious Life Review*, July–Aug. Republished (1997) in *American Benedictine Review*, June.

8   *Dial.* II, 1:6–7.

9   Nugent, A. (1999), "Benedict: A Sense of Prayer" in *American Benedictine Review*, June, pp. 149–160.

10 See Luckman and Kulzer, *Op. cit.*

11 Guigo 11, *Scala Claustralium* 2. On the whole topic of *Lectio Divina*, see Casey, M. (1996), *Sacred Reading: The Ancient Art of Lectio Divina*, Missouri: Ligouri.

12 Casey, *Op. cit.*

13 Gregory the Great, *Dialogues* III, 16.

3

CARMELITE SPIRITUALITY

Wilfrid McGreal, OCarm

History and Tradition

The Carmelite story begins around the year 1200 with a group of hermits living on Mount Carmel. The hermits were originally pilgrims who had come from Western Europe urged on by a quest to encounter the Jesus of the Gospels. They were poor men, rich in faith and energised by powerful love. The hermits were not to live long on Mount Carmel, as the course of history would bring them back to Europe. However, the vision that began this story is still alive today and the 800-year story can be expressed by what we now describe as the Carmelite tradition of spirituality.

These hermits were part of the evangelical awakening that marked the course of Christianity in Western Europe in the 12th century. The 12th century was a time of growth and prosperity in Europe and as more people had access to learning, so a thirst grew for a greater knowledge of Christ and His teaching. A whole host of groups sprang up eager for a deepening of faith and a more radical living of the Gospel. The genius of the Church's hierarchy allowed it to harness this thirst for God and so revitalise the Church. The most influential of these groups were the Franciscans, but it was the organisational gift of St Dominic that helped to give a structure to such inspirational gifts. The first Carmelites, the hermits on Carmel, were part of this movement. They wanted to follow Christ as his disciples and their pilgrimage as poor men to the Holy Land allowed them to live inspired by the example of the first Christian community in Jerusalem.

The first Carmelites were hermits, poor men, brothers who shared God's word with the people. They had chosen to live on Mount Carmel, which is close to the modern town of Haifa. Seen from the sea, it is a gentle green ridge no more than 2,000 feet high. On the landward side it is scarred by small valleys with streams and pools scattered among the rock. The first Carmelites settled in one of these sheltered spots near the fountain of Elijah – the Wadi Am-es-Sah. Jacques de Vitry, Bishop of Acre, wrote about 1216:

> *Others after the example of the holy solitary Elijah, the prophet, lived as hermits in the beehives of small cells on Mount Carmel . . . near the spring which is called the Spring of Elijah.*[1]

By the end of the first decade of the 13th century, these hermits realised that they needed help to structure their lives and they approached Albert, Patriarch of Jerusalem, for a way of life. As they were still viewed as a group of laymen, they were given a way of life rather than a rule. However, Albert's action recognised them as a community and his legislation was to be confirmed by Gregory IX in 1229. In 1247, Innocent IV confirmed the text as a Rule in the Bull *Quem Honorem Conditoris*. The Papal approval of the Rule was also to effect a change in the lives of the hermits, drawing them into the mendicant way of life.

The *Rule of St Albert*, as it has come to be known, is a concise document but it is rich in meaning and crucial for any understanding of Carmelite spirituality. What is at the heart of the *Rule*? What does it have to say today?

The essence of the *Rule* is the desire to live a life of allegiance to Jesus Christ, serving the Lord with a pure heart and a clear conscience. The most recent edition of the *Constitutions of the Order* state that Carmelites live their life of allegiance to Christ through a commitment to seek the face of the living God through community and through service in the midst of the people. Jesus Christ claimed the total allegiance of the first Carmelites as they strove to work for the deepest living of the Gospel and all for which Jesus stood. There is also the image of a struggle — not just the spiritual warfare of Paul's writing but also the vision of John's Gospel, where light will not be overcome by the dark and truth is the source of freedom. Carmel is a space for growth and it is also a place of struggle. It was on Carmel that Elijah overcame the priests of Baal and vindicated the living God.

Faithfulness to Christ is enhanced for a Carmelite by a love of His law — His Word. Reflecting night and day is central to this project. It is this attitude of listening, pondering God's Word in Scripture, that is at the heart of a Carmelite's life.

The Rule

The concrete living out of the *Rule* is achieved by obeying the Prior. However, the Prior was to exercise his authority as Christ would have done — as a servant. The Prior is the servant of the community, helping everyone to reach their common goal of faithfulness to Christ.

In the important working out of the relationship between the Prior and the community, an interchange of ideas and aspirations must be to the fore. The brothers are to meet to discuss key issues and then the Prior ensures that whatever has been agreed is put into practice. The Prior welcomes visitors, ensuring that hospitality and the needs of the community are not in conflict. In his role of service, the Prior is often the conscience or memory of the community.

In any attempt to understand or live the *Rule*, there can be conflict between its eremitical aspect and the community dimension. Such interpretations can be culturally conditioned or come through a particular focus. Again, it is often easier to posit an opposition than to work towards a creative unity which will still often have its own tensions.

Some commentators have taken Chapter 7 to be at the heart of the *Rule*:

> *Each one of you is to stay in his own cell or*
> *nearby, pondering the Lord's Law day and*
> *night and keeping watch in prayer unless at-*
> *tending to some other duty.*[2]

This envisages an engagement of the mind and heart where a brother is being so absorbed by the Scriptures that God's Word is in his heart and mind at all times. The solitude and silence that surrounds the Carmelite enables the focus to be on God and God's Word. However, even from the earliest days of the Carmelite project, the brothers left their solitude to preach and share their love of God's Word with people. From 1247 onwards, they had opted for the mendicant life, which in principle meant mobility and association with the growing urban culture of Western Europe. In the context of a commitment to the apostolate as well as eremitical life, meditation came to mean an ever-deepening reflection on the Scriptures, so that people at large could be helped by their insight and preaching. The brother is also expected to be vigilant in prayer so that he is ready to welcome the Lord when he comes again. A consequence of this vigilance is a growth in sensitivity in being aware that we must not allow our hearts to grow coarse or lessen the ardour of our love for our neighbour. Later chapters of the *Rule*, with their focus on spiritual warfare and commitment to fraternal living, give a more focused realisation of the call to vigilant prayer.

However, the overall tenor of this chapter is to praise and value the solitude that enables prayer, but not in the sense of a flight from life; rather to gain the energy, focus and vitality to work with people and, above all, to practise love as brothers in community at the service of other people.

Given these considerations, modern commentators on the *Rule* have suggested that the heart of the *Rule* is not just Chapter 7, but Chapters 7 to 11. The *Rule* does not just envisage isolated persons praying in their cells, but rather a community who journeyed in unity. Here we can feel the inspiration of the Acts of the Apostles depicting the early Christians in Jerusalem. These chapters take us from solitude to a celebration of praise as the Psalms are prayed in common. There is a sharing of goods, an openness to poverty and also a sharing of ideals and needs in regular meetings. All this culminates in the celebration of daily Eucharist. If anything is at the heart of the *Rule*, it is the daily celebration of the Eucharist and the brotherly communion that it achieves.

The following of Christ, the great project of the *Rule*, is achieved by becoming a community of disciples who owe everything to Christ, but above all their allegiance. Discipleship in a community means that the Carmelite lives in Christ. It means that the *Rule* is not interested in an individualistic spirituality, but rather in the realisation of an ecclesial communion. The reflecting on God's world in solitude energises and leads to community in Eucharist and then to the living out of that love with one's brother. The fraternity that grows from this prayer and celebration is not severe or harshly ascetic, nor is it over-enthusiastic. The *Rule* has no place for penalties, but envisages the interaction of community meetings and the role of the Prior as a servant brother. A freedom to serve emerges from this dynamic love and from the encounter with God that comes from pondering His Word in the heart.

Spirit of the Desert

An energy and symbol that is found in the Carmelite *Rule* is Jerusalem. The journey to Jerusalem was the original inspiration of the first Carmelites. However, the central chapters of the *Rule* are obviously inspired by the vision of the Jerusalem community found in Acts, chapters 2 and 4, a community of disciples who were fervent in prayer, sharing all in common and bonded by the breaking of bread. The first Jerusalem community was a community of prayer and a community that attracted others by the quality of its being. The Carmelite *Rule* is shaped and inspired by that ideal, an ideal that is always being called into being in every generation.

In considering the place of the *Rule* in Carmelite spirituality, it is important to see how history shaped it. The first hermits gradually evolved into a community so that they combined eremitic elements with the life of a community. What was to be a challenging shaping element was the adoption of mendicancy when circumstances drove them to Europe around 1240. The Carmelites had sprung from the same renewal movement and so they felt an attraction to adopting a way of life shaped by poverty and at the service of the people. However, the combining of the three elements of the eremitical, community and mendicant has led to ten-

sions, tensions first felt in the 13th century and still
there today. But as a Dutch commentator on the *Rule*
has pointed out, "they have forced Carmelites to go below the surface, to a deeper level, to look for the mystical space of contemplation".[3]

The move from the Holy Land to Europe and the
implications of the mendicant way of life caused 13th-
century Carmelites to reflect on their origins and to look
for symbols that would express the essence of their vision. Leaving Mount Carmel and the solitude it stood
for meant that the desert was to be a space in the heart
and the mountain took on the imagery of the journey
that had to be achieved. So despite the fact of foundations being made in towns and the brethren, like Dominicans and Franciscans, being involved in university
life, there was still a deep sense of solitude, silence and
the desert. The *Rule* speaks of spiritual warfare and that
struggle goes on in the desert. If the desert is carefully
tended, it flourishes. By this is meant not so much a
physical space, but rather the geography of the heart.
Silence and solitude combine to create the conditions
where God can be all in all. John Welch expresses this
inner beauty and transfiguration:

> *A desert carefully tended becomes a garden. In
> the imagination of Carmelites, Mount Carmel
> represents not only the solitude in which the
> hermit wrestles demons, but it also represents
> the flowering of new, verdant life. The invitation
> to Carmel offered by the tradition is an invita-
> tion to open one's life to the loving activity of God*

*and so to the blossoming of one's life. The garden
is a counter-symbol to the desert. Mount Carmel
represented solitude and stark battle to the Carmelite, but it was also a place of physical beauty
which offered fresh water, thick forest, striking
vistas, and the company of wild animals.*[4]

It is in this context of change and tension that Nicholas
the Frenchman appears. He was Prior General from
1266–1271. From his writing, it is evident that he was a
person of some learning, with a familiarity not just of
the Scriptures, but also with Aristotle and other classical writers. He visited the various provinces of the Order from England to Sicily and was well acquainted with
what was afoot. It would seem that he had lived as a
hermit and was none too pleased with the movement
towards the active life. He wrote a passionate treatise,
The Flaming Arrow, a moving appeal to the brothers to
return to the spirit of the desert.

It seems that his plea found little support and in
1271 Nicholas resigned his office of Prior General. The
treatise is not so much an attack on the apostolic life as
a caring criticism of those who would take up the apostolate without preparation and foresight. There was a
need for prayerful responsibility and a sense of how ex-
acting the apostolate could be. It was not enough to feel
the urge to preach, there was the need to be properly
formed: education was a prerequisite. Interestingly, by
the next decade, Carmelites were taking their place in
the universities.

Nicholas, however, in his treatise articulated a problem that is in the end common to all Christians — how
can a vision of the desert, a sense of solitude, be combined with apostolic activity? Nicholas did not see them
as incompatible but issued a challenge to work out a
creative synthesis, one that would require sensitivity
and discipline in its realisation. However, the final impression that Nicholas leaves is one of being overwhelmed by the challenge, by the change. The evolution
of the Carmelite story has responded to the challenge,
even though at times it could have seemed to have been
misguided. The wonder has been that in the unravelling
of the story, human inconsistency has been answered by
God's faithfulness.

Elijah

By the late 13th century, Carmelites were asking questions about their origins that would help develop their
vision, their spirituality, and it would see Mary and
Elijah emerge as symbolic figures. The first recorded
attempt to answer questions about Carmelite origins is
found in the opening lines of the *Constitutions of the
Order* drawn up in London in 1281.

> *We declare, bearing testimony to the truth, that
> from the time when the prophets Elijah and
> Elisha dwelt devoutly on Mount Carmel, holy
> Fathers both of the Old and New Testament,
> whom the contemplation of heavenly things
> drew to the solitude of the same mountain, have
> without doubt led praiseworthy lives there by*

> *the fountain of Elijah in holy penitence unceas-*
> *ingly and successfully maintained.*
>
> *It was these same successors whom Albert the*
> *Patriarch of Jerusalem in the time of Innocent III*
> *united into a community, writing a rule for them*
> *which Pope Honorius, the successor of the same*
> *Innocent, and many of their successors, approv-*
> *ing this Order, most devoutly confirmed by their*
> *charters. In the profession of this rule, we, their*
> *followers, serve the Lord in diverse parts of the*
> *world, even to the present day.* [5]

This is the seed from which the tradition of Elijah was to grow. Elijah as the one who stood before God in prayer, witnessing to truth before the powerful, reso-nated with late 13th-century Carmelites as they tried to bridge the hermit and mendicant traditions. Elijah is also a man on a journey not to Jerusalem but still to the East, to the brook Cherith where God is experienced.

The Carmelite tradition about Elijah and, to a lesser extent, about Mary is found in the *Liber de Institutione Primorum Monachorum.*[6] The document was com-posed by Felip Biot, a Catalonian Carmelite, about 1370. The *Institute* is, after the *Rule*, a key work in under-standing Carmelite spirituality and would have influ-enced Teresa of Avila and John of the Cross. The Australian Carmelite, Paul Chandler, has done much to make this document available to the contemporary reader. It contains all the key themes of Carmelite spiri-tuality: allegiance to Christ, openness to Scriptures, the sense of silence and solitude and the undivided heart.

Marian elements also emerge, but above all there is an underlying sense of God's presence and protection found in intimate prayer. The work is full of symbols — the mountain, the desert, the brook Cherith and the little cloud that prefigures Mary.

The work is a synthesis of older Carmelite traditions and the way Carmelites of that period read Scripture. What is crucial is the way it came to colour Carmelite thinking about the very essence of the Order and above all it is the expression of the Elijah tradition.

Paul Chandler raises an issue about the work that helps our understanding in a most positive way. He sees in these writings the early Carmelite imagination constructing a myth. The role of myth is always valuable and in a religious context myth has profound significance. It is the way the Community reflects on the key experiences that shape them so that the experiences can then be handed on as a formative story:

> *In this work we are able to observe the medieval Carmelite imagination at work in the construction of a myth. This myth expresses the order's sense of the nature and purpose of its vocation in the church and gives imaginative form to the values and aspirations which it wished to see expressed in its life as a religious community. Its principal building blocks are the Scriptures, which are ingeniously interpreted to construct a continuous history of the "Elijah institute" over the centuries from the time of its foundation by the prophet until his followers*

were converted to Christianity. Our first reaction may be to laugh at this apparent naïveté, but a more careful and sympathetic reading will show a profound spiritual dynamic at work. The essential elements and ideals of Carmelite life — the inspiration of the Spirit, the opening of the heart and mind to the Messiah, the dynamic of communal discernment, the importance of the word of God, and much else besides — are projected into the past and given concrete "mythic" form. Once we have the key to interpreting these stories, we can see unfold the spiritual itinerary of the Carmelite and the inner dynamic and central values of the Carmelite vocation.[7]

In the 21st century, Carmelites continue to reflect on Elijah but now would see him as passionate for truth, one who has encountered God and proclaims that vision. Carmelites realise that Elijah was a champion of the poor and the oppressed. As the one who cared for the widow and the poor, Elijah has helped Carmelites discover a solidarity with the poor. However, in the light of recent events Carmelites see Elijah who encountered God on Horeb as one who proclaims truth about God and would prevent us manipulating God's name for political ends. Carmelites would pray that Elijah can speak to Jews, Muslims and Christians in a special way in the shadow of the events of September 2001.

Mary

The *Institute* also links the Elijan and Marian traditions
of the Order. Mary is seen as a caring presence, as a Pa-
troness; because of the deep empathy that the early
Carmelites felt for Mary, they were able to see her as
sister, a fellow disciple who, like them, pondered the
Word of God, anxious to bring Jesus to a waiting world.

One expression of Mary as patron of the Order is the
scapular devotion. The origins of this devotion are ob-
scure. Links are made with St Simon Stock and 13th-
century England, but historians have never been able to
reach a satisfactory conclusion. However, this devotion
has flourished in the Church since the late Middle Ages.
Popular devotions with their symbolic content have a
great value, as they are a powerful way of communication that touches the imagination.

Many Carmelites today would say that the Order's
basic intuition about Mary has always been her presence. There has always been a sense of Mary's closeness, a sense that she is the one who has protected the
Order. Again, the title "sister" underlines a warmth that
values Mary as a person rather than a role.

Time of Reform

During the late Middle Ages, the Carmelite story is one
of growth, of active involvement in the ministry of
preaching and university life. However, the vision of the
desert and the sense of solitude was never lost. While
some Carmelites fell away from the spirit of the *Rule*,
reform movements kept the vision alive. The establish-

ment of convents for women under the leadership of
John Soreth was a landmark and the 550th anniversary
of the Bull *Cum Nulla* is being celebrated in 2002.

Renewal in the Order and a deepening of the understanding of the Carmelite story came not through legislation but through the vision and inspiration of John of
the Cross and Teresa of Avila. John and Teresa provided the impetus for renewal in the Order and left a
wonderful legacy for Christianity as a whole. They represent both continuity and a way forward in the Carmelite story.

The 16th century was a time of change and creativ-
ity. It was the era of discovery, the Renaissance and the
Reformation. It was also an era of religious and political
control, with the Inquisition casting a shadow over the
lives of both Teresa and John.

Teresa of Avila

Teresa had entered the Convent of the Incarnation at
Avila when she was 20 years old in 1535. A turning
point came in her life in 1554 when she was touched to
the core of her being at the realisation of Christ's suffering and wounded humanity. She began to think about
the possibility of beginning a reform in Carmel, seeing
that as part of the renewal needed by the Church of that
time. She was aware of the ideals of Carmel expressed
in the *Rule* and the *Institute* and she summed up these
ideals when she said:

○   *So I say now that all of us who wear this holy
    habit of Carmel are called to prayer and con-
    templation. This call explains our origin; we
    are descendants of men who felt this call, of
    those holy fathers on Mount Carmel who in
    such great solitude and contempt for the world
    sought this treasure, this precious pearl of con-
    templation that we are speaking about. Yet few
    of us dispose ourselves that the Lord may com-
    municate it to us.*[8]

She wanted to restore the life of prayer in solitude — she
wanted to find the essence of life on Mount Carmel. Her
vision was of a small community bonded by friendship
and a simple lifestyle. It was this vision and her experiences in prayer that she began to write down so that she
could share her intimacy with Christ with her sisters.

○   For Teresa, the inner journey is one where the love
and mercy of God transform her. However, she does
this while being very conscious that the way forward is
to allow her humanity to be transformed and linked to
the humanity of Christ. She is quite blunt in opposing
those who would intellectualise prayer life. "We are not
angels, we have a body". Teresa was a person who had a
gift for friendship and it was this gift that was lifted up
and transformed through her understanding that Jesus
Christ was her good friend. Teresa wants to spend time
with that friend in a conversation, which is for her the
best way of prayer. The more she is in friendship, the
more God's mercy and grace water the garden of her
being. Like the picture of Elijah in the *Institute*, she

drinks from the source of God's love. She journeys to the summit, which is union with Christ, and it is to this summit that Teresa believes all are called. Teresa has the sense that what she experiences in prayer — the mercy, the friendship, intimacy with Christ — should be normal for all of us. We will have dryness, we will feel absence, but in that experience we are being drawn out of ourselves to a new stage of union.

Teresa wrote with frankness; she was not a theologian and never pretended to be one. She was not a biblical scholar; access to the Bible was not easy, as even Spanish versions of the Scriptures were not readily available. However, she was conscious of God giving her words and she felt that her experience, her testimony, had a validity and she was happy to share her experience. This desire to help others in their journey, especially her sisters in St Joseph, is the inspiration behind the *Way of Perfection*. It is meant to be a help in teaching her sisters to pray and reflects where Teresa had reached in her journey. As a Carmelite, she was committed to following Christ, being in allegiance, given over to her Lord. Living a life of greater solitude in St Joseph's where she could live Chapter 7 of the *Rule*, pondering God's word, opened her ever more to receiving Christ in the most profound way. She was able to open herself more and more so that Christ could be everything for her. Christ becomes for her the teacher of prayer who enables us to pray to the Father from the depth of our being. Images abound in her writings, many of them coming from Carmelite sources like springs of living water and the reality of spiritual warfare. The *Rule* and the Elijah myth provide the framework, the original inspiration.

Love of neighbour means friendship and the warmth of human friendship is Teresa's keynote. An essential part of her reform was to create communities where the human dimension was respected and where the sisters lived in friendship. Teresa opposed notions of rank and knew from her own family's experience how notions of honour, status and race were damaging and unchristian. Her communities were truly sisterhoods where people could live accepting each other and growing through an intimate sharing of life.

Friendship with God, entry into the life of the Trinity is the end of the journey in the *Way of Perfection*. Teresa is conscious of the nearness of God, the one who takes the initiative. Again, it is the humanity of Christ as found in the Gospel that is the way for Teresa. Christ is the teacher and the "Our Father" is the great prayer that he gives us. For Teresa, this prayer, prayed with recollection, allowing it to be the starting point for contemplation, makes it the gateway to closeness with God. Then, in the closeness to God, through Christ we are nourished with springs of living water.

It was at this stage in her life in 1567 that Teresa encountered John Baptist Rossi, the Prior General of the Order, who was visiting the Spanish Provinces. Rossi was eager to continue the project of reform that his predecessor Nicholas Audet had begun. However, while Rossi was committed to structural reform, Teresa's project offered something that went far beyond legal prescriptions. She wanted the following of Christ with an undivided heart, the vision of the "way of life" of Albert. Teresa was nervous when she met the Prior General, thinking he might be angry with her or send her back to the Incarnation. The opposite was true, as Rossi saw that Teresa had vision and her way had a significance for the whole Order. He took her work under his jurisdiction and encouraged its propagation. Rossi was to write to Teresa urging her to found as many convents as there were hairs on her head. Teresa and Rossi established a deep respect for each other. In fact, he was to write in 1569 to the nuns at Medina Del Campo saying:

> *I give infinite thanks to the Divine Majesty for the great favour bestowed on this Order by the diligence and goodness of Our Reverend Mother Teresa of Jesus. She profits the Order more than all the friars in Spain. I admonish all to obey the above mentioned Teresa as a true superior and a jewel to be much valued as precious and a friend of God.*[9]

John of the Cross

It was about this time that Teresa met a young Carmelite friar, John of the Cross, who was to carry her renewal among the friars. To say that Teresa was a shaping influence on John does nothing to deny his special genius. Teresa's friendship with John enabled him to find that freedom to grow and express his experiences of prayer and closeness to God. However, John was also formed in a school of suffering because misunderstandings and Church politics led to his unjust imprisonment. However, prison was a time of deep encounter with God and that encounter was beautifully expressed in his poems.

John's deep sense of union with the Divine is often called mystical. It was, as the *Institute* had said, a tasting of the reality of God even in this life. If anyone wants to learn from John of the Cross, it is important to approach him in the first place through his poetry and then come to peruse the long prose commentaries. His poems are wonderful lyrical pieces written with great economy of style. John said that he did not have to search for words and images, they just came. Certainly, the *Dark Night* and the *Spiritual Canticle* reflect his reading of Scripture and above all his love of the Song of Songs. This is a poetic book of the Bible that sings of the beauty and goodness of human loving. It is rich in imagery and is not afraid to be sensuous and erotic. The poetry is totally open in its celebration of sexual love, but is in no way prurient. The *Dark Night* and the *Spiritual Canticle* speak of the yearning of the lover's heart for the beloved. The gaze of God, the beloved, wounds the lover who then can only find satisfaction when healed by loving union. This desire for God that can only be fulfilled by union echoes the *Rule*, and the sense of journeying is like Elijah moving to the east to the source of life at Cherith.

John also wrote four great prose works that are both commentaries on his poems and a vision of how we achieve union with God. The four works are *The Ascent* of Mount Carmel, *The Dark Night, Spiritual Canticle* and *The Living Flame of Love*. Written between 1579 and 1586, they were meant to help the friars and nuns of the Reform.

John introduces the concept of the "dark night" early on as the way a person grows closer to God. He points out that what he has to say will not be easy and apologises for his "awkward style", and he stresses that he is writing for people who are already taking all this very seriously — the friars and nuns of the Reform.

It needs to be made quite clear that John saw the "dark night" as being initiated by God, but that does not mean that the individual concerned is totally passive in the process. Another aspect of the "dark night" is the way a person so affected has the feeling that God seems to be absent; it is important to recognise that this is a seeming absence of God. It is not as if God has withdrawn from a person's life. Again, it needs to be noted that not everyone in their journey to God passes through the "dark night". In an attempt to understand what John means by the "dark night", the reader must always remember that the person who has entered this process has to play his or her part. John would not want to deny our basic freedom or our use of reason.

The way of the night is for John the way of *nada*. A time of faith, a time of purification, *nada* is an escape from all that is negative so that a person finds their all — *todo* — in God. The way of the night is both a process that we can co-operate in by positive creative practices, but it also involves being open to God working in us. It

is a time of maturity but should be lived in a spirit of
trust. However, once a person comes closer to God in
faith, then in the new relationship it is possible to live
life with greater humanity and enjoy creation from a
more positive perspective. John in his own life loved
nature and had wonderful friendships. Most of his cor-
respondence has been lost, but what survives reveals a
man of warmth, loyalty and integrity. His closeness to
God helped his growth in humanity.

Obviously the joy of coming into a close relationship
with God is something that few people can articulate.
John's poems do that through powerful symbols and
because he was able to find words that even surprised
him by their power. However, what stands out in John's
writings is the language he uses about our union with
God. It is the language and images of the most tender
and fulfilled human loving. This is powerful news for
our own times because it is telling us that human love at
its most sublime is the best image we can find for the
relationship between God and ourselves. It also suggests that we need some experience of human tenderness
to set us on the journey to God. I believe that how we
love each other and how we love God is reciprocal, each
love affecting and enhancing the other. The journey into
God that John shows us is a journey where possessive-
ness disappears and faith, trust and love find freedom to
flourish. It is because a certain true human growth and
freedom is realised that we can come close to God. If,
however, we have grown to a true maturity in our inner-

most being, then we are able to relate in a way that is gentler, deeper and more understanding of the other.

The vision and gifts that flowed from John and Teresa renewed Carmel and enriched the Church as a whole. They are two great teachers, gifted with imaginative powers and humanity.

Thérèse of Lisieux

Any telling of the Carmelite story must focus on the brief but significant life of Thérèse of Lisieux. She has recently been declared a Doctor of the Church. Her gift was to renew the bond between spirituality and theology and to reaffirm the value of the mystical. She transcended the many elements of the late 19th-century French bourgeois life that affected the Carmel at Lisieux. She was the author of her own life, full of originality. The Carmel at Lisieux lacked the spirit of Teresa of Avila with the *Rule* being lived with a strictness that missed its essential humanity. Her lively imagination links her to Teresa of Avila and in the last months of her life, during her final illness, she lived out the passive night in the spirit of John of the Cross.

Thérèse stands at the centre of the Carmelite tradition with her belief that we can all achieve closeness to God through our prayer, our following of Jesus Christ as we live the Gospel. This is her teaching on the "Little Way". For Thérèse, holiness, closeness to God, is not achieved by spectacular ascetic practices. We come to God by infusing love into every aspect of life. The "Little Way" is one of childlike trust in God, but it is not infantile and naïve, or a searching for the lost innocence of some idealised childhood. Thérèse had known through childhood and early adolescence the pain of separation from those she loved. She wanted a quiet hidden relationship, living out in secret her love for God. This "Little Way" was a reaction to strictness and the spectacular ascetic practices that seemed to be demanded by her Prioress.

This trust was tested during her final illness. She felt as if she was in total darkness and that her belief was an illusion. This was a time of immense desolation, even to the point of thinking that suicide would end the pain and the sense of futility. Thérèse has much to teach us from her experience of terminal illness; what emerges is that even in the darkness she could cling onto a sense that we are never abandoned by God. It was in the midst of her suffering that she had a moment of insight and light that helped her express the meaning of her life and her vocation. Reading St Paul and aware of the mystical body of Christ, she realised that love alone mattered and that her calling was to be love in the heart of the Church. This insight gave her a generous sense of the Church and enhanced her awareness of the Communion of Saints.

Thérèse's greatness is her ability to grasp that the Christian life is the realisation of love in the community where you live. However, that community, if inspired by the dynamic of love, will always be open and creative. She realised that the call to love was linked to the same obedience that brought Jesus to the Cross. Her last months were a painful journey to Jerusalem and her

Calvary. Like Jesus, she came to the end in a time of terrible darkness and in this she fulfilled her faithful following, her allegiance to Jesus. By faith she grasped the meaning of the heavenly Jerusalem and yet at times in her last months she felt as if that reality could be snatched away from her, that her hope might even be in vain. We know she kept journeying and in the end peace broke through the darkness and the pain.

However, the great contribution, the message that Thérèse has for us today, is of the immense self-sacrificing love that Christ has for his community. By her life, Thérèse became an icon of that love and shows us a face of the Church that is more than the institution. The writer Chris O'Donnell is influenced by the theology of Von Balthasar when he says that Thérèse has something vital to teach the post-Vatican II Church. If we want a renewed and missionary Church, we need to move away from mere organisational and structural changes and live love. We will then see the wonderful reality of the Communion of Saints and learn to understand how much worth there is in an act of pure love — in living the "Little Way". In her discipleship, Thérèse is in many ways a wonderful window into the faith of Mary, whose unconditional trust lived through Calvary and then experienced the fullness of the Resurrection.

In *Ephesians*, Paul speaks of us all as being "God's work of art". Thérèse is an immortal diamond, crafted by love in her suffering and in her creative way of living life. She was wonderfully inserted in the Carmelite tradition, living the *Rule* and loving the Scriptures. Like

Elijah, she too journeyed to her own meeting with God. Like the prophet, she came to the end of her tether, yet was fed and enabled to carry on. The prophet encountered God in the Wadi Cherith and on Horeb. Thérèse journeyed with Christ and came to the eternal mountain Sion and the New Jerusalem.

A Contemporary Relevance

The question can be asked: what does the 800-year-old story of Carmel, its journey and its symbols, have to say to the 21st century? The events of September 11th, 2001, have shaken the world and yet, on another level, left it unchanged. Our culture, our way of life, is still lived very much on the surface and the capacity of the human heart to wonder, search and listen is much affected. What is worrying is the way compassion is dismissed as being weakness rather than the way the power of God is shown in reckless mercy. People know they have needs but in the restless search too often a focus is lacking and if the answer is not instant, the search is called off. The restlessness and frustration can also end up in reactions that are self-destructive and violent.

Our world needs a sense of community and a genuine hope that its wounds can be healed. Perhaps the skill, the strategy that needs to be rediscovered is the ability to listen. Listening, pondering, treasuring in the heart are values that matter to Carmelites. The *Rule* asks Carmelites to immerse themselves in the Scriptures and by doing this they are opened to the presence of the mystery that is God.

A steady listening, attentiveness to the mystery, is contemplation. The prerequisites for such listening are solitude and silence. We need to find a place and a time to stop and to be, rather than merely to do. However, listening in silence and openness to the mystery that is God is not meant to make us self-absorbed or feel superior. The light that comes from listening gives us energy to move away from egoism. We see what can be, or have become, the false gods and idols in our lives. This freedom from lesser gods is what is meant by purity of heart, which is an important element in the Carmelite tradition. It means that we desire to live in allegiance to Jesus Christ and to his work, which is the establishment of the Kingdom of God. A pure heart means that, as we become aware of the free gift of God's love, then we will want to love others in a way that is truly liberating, life-enhancing and respectful of human dignity. We have received freely from God's generosity, therefore we want to respond to that love and give thanks to it by helping others into the banquet of life. As Gustavo Gutiérrez said, "Mystical language expresses the gratuitousness of God's love, prophetic language expresses the demands this love makes whole".[10]

However, for Carmelites, the imperative of prayer that asks us to love and serve others as God loves us finds its initial expression in community life. From the first days on Carmel, the brothers came out of their solitude to meet, to celebrate Eucharist and to grow in understanding together. In a society that is so often violent, fragmented and far from peace, the poetry of people who live together in a community of friendship is a potent sign. A real community of friendship is a healing reality for others and also an antidote to the scramble for power, wealth and money. In our own day, unbridled capitalism has become, as Pope John Paul II suggests, a new "fascism", with currency speculators blighting economies and making the poor poorer. On a personal level, consumerism as a way of life tears the heart out of our relationships. I *become* the Gucci, the car, the house and the holiday. However, where brothers and sisters share life in simplicity and love, hope may emerge. When Teresa of Avila renewed Carmel, she saw the quality of human relationships as the key test. The ideal she proclaimed was, "All must be friends, all must be loved, all must be held dear, all must be helped". If we are a community of friendship and simplicity our energy will be freed to work for justice.

Listening, recognising the wisdom of the heart brings us to that contemplative stage that opens us to God's loving presence. The closer we are to God, the more we live God's qualities, above all his mercy. It is this growth in compassion, flowing from prayer, that could be so life-enhancing for a world in turmoil. Our gratitude towards God is best shown in our sensitive love for others. The love we receive from God is, as St Thérèse said, all free — "It is all grace". So our response should be characterised by generosity. Spirituality is not a cosy option but is the call to respond to God's love by our involvement in what can be a dark and difficult world. We need to go into the desert of love, into a night of trust.

Perhaps a final word about the Carmelite story and the place of its tradition of spirituality for today should come from the Order's *Constitutions*. This document, published in 1996, is a contemporary reflection on the *Rule*, expressing insights that flow from the ancient tradition.

In the Scriptures and in Carmelite tradition,
the prophet Elijah is respected as the one
who in various ways knew how to read the new
   signs of the presence of God
and who was able, not least,
to reconcile those who had become strangers or
   enemies.
As Carmelites, heartened by this example
and by our strong desire to put into practice our
   Lord's teachings
of love and reconciliation,
we shall take part in the ecumenical movement
and in inter-religious dialogue,
promoted by the Second Vatican Council.
Through the former we shall promote relationships
with the Orthodox and other Christians.
Through the latter we shall promote dialogue at
   various levels
with Jews and Muslims,
with whom we share devotion to the prophet
   Elijah as a man of God;
we shall enter into dialogue also with Hindus
   and Buddhists
and those of other religions.

Moreover, Carmelites are to make themselves
   available
to accompany those who genuinely desire

*to experience the transcendent in their lives
or who wish to share their experience of God.*[11]

Notes

[1]   Smet, J. OCarm (1988), *The Carmelites,* Vol. 1, Illinois: Carmelite Spiritual Centre, p. 3.

[2]   Clarke, H. and Edwards, B. (eds.) (1973), *The Rule of St Albert,* Aylesford & Kensington, p. 83.

[3]   Waayman, K. (1999), *The Mystical Space of Carmel,* Leuven: Peeters, p. 99.

[4]   Welch, J. (1996), *The Carmelite Way,* Gracewing, p. 28.

[5]   Staring, A. (1989), *Medieval Carmelite Heritage,* Rome: Carmelite Institute, p. 40.

[6]   Chandler, P. *Liber de Institutione Primorum Monachorum*, Draft translation.

[7]   Chandler, P. (1991), *A Journey with Elijah,* Rome: Carmelite Institute, p. 14.

[8]   Kavanaugh, K. and Rodriguez, O. (1980), *Interior Castle* in *Collected Works of St Teresa of Avila*, Vol. 2, Washington: ICS Publications, p. 335.

[9]   Zimmerman B. (1936), *Regesta John Baptist Rossi,* Rome, pp. 88–89.

[10] Gutiérrez, G. (1987), *Job,* Claretian Publications, p. 95.

[11] *Carmelite Constitutions* (1996), Victoria, Australia: Carmelite Publications, p. 51.

Further Reading

Kavanaugh, K. and Rodriguez, O. (1980), *Collected Works of St Teresa of Avila*, 3 volumes, Washington: ICS Publications.

Kavanaugh, K. and Rodriguez, O. (1991), *Collected Works of St John of the Cross*, Washington: ICS Publications.

McGreal, W. (1999), *At the Fountain of Elijah*, London: DLT.

O'Donnell, C. (1997), *Love in the Heart of the Church*, Dublin: Veritas.

Slattery, P. (1991), *The Springs of Carmel*, New York: Alba House.

Welch, J. (1996), *The Carmelite Way*, Leominster: Gracewing Fowler Wright.

Williams, R. (1991), *Teresa of Avila*, Harrisburg, PA: Morehouse Publishing.

4

CISTERCIAN SPIRITUALITY

Fr Nivard Kinsella, OCSO

History

The Cistercians came into being in 1098, with the foundation of the monastery of Cîteaux, about 20 kilometres from the city of Dijon. This was the century of what is known as The Gregorian Reform, inspired by the reforming efforts of Pope Gregory VII (1073–1085). The period saw many efforts at renewing monastic life — the Camaldolese monks and the Carthusians emerged at this time. The ideals of solitude, separation from the world and poverty were stressed. Several of these reforming movements were nearer to the ideal of the Desert Fathers than to the mainstream of European monastic history, and a number of them did not survive. Eventually what we might call the second wave of monastic reform took place with the realisation of the value of the *Rule of St Benedict*, which was the mainstream of European monasticism. The values the reformers were seeking could be found in the *Rule of*

Benedict, which had formed monastic life in Europe since the 6th century.

The monastery of Molesmes in Burgundy was a traditional Benedictine house. A group of about 25 monks left Molesmes to found a new reformed monastery, under the leadership of Robert, the Abbot, Alberic the Prior, and Stephen Harding, an Englishman. Robert eventually returned to Molesmes and was succeeded as Abbot of "The New Monastery" by Alberic, who died in 1109. The Community then elected Stephen and his influence on the shape of the reform was the most important. He wrote *The Charter of Charity*, outlining the relations between the Abbeys of the Reform, and prescribing an annual General Chapter of the Abbots.

The aim of the Cistercian Reform was "to be poor with the poor Christ" and this led to a simpler liturgy, a determination to live by the work of the monks, having no income from parishes or benefices of any kind, and a simplification of the life of the monks, with regard to food, clothing and general lifestyle. The monasteries would not have schools or parishes, and the monks would support themselves by manual work. Separation from secular society was stressed and manual labour was regarded as very important. While the liturgy was simplified, it still took up a good deal of time in the day, and it soon became apparent that the monks could not both attend choir and do the amount of farm work needed to keep the monastery in being. As a result, Lay Brothers were instituted. While the idea was not completely original to the Cistercians, it was they who effectively made the idea work.

Lay Brothers

The Lay Brothers were men who were not bound to the full choir offices and who devoted most of their day to manual work. At the same time, it is important to realise that they were not merely workmen living in the monastery. They lived a strictly regulated community life, under the direction of a choir monk — the Master of the Lay Brothers. They took the same vows as the monks, attended some of the offices, and had regular conferences and direction from the Master. They were in effect monks without the obligation of full choir attendance. As the monasteries increased in number and the fame of the monks grew, many a landowner made donations of land to them on condition they would pray for himself and his family. Often these lands were extensive and were a considerable distance from the monastery, so a group of Lay Brothers sometimes lived at these out-farms, which were known as Granges.

The institution of Lay Brothers opened the monastic life to men who would not be able to take on the choir duties as they lacked a clerical education, and in this way a new chapter of monastic life was begun. It also provided a large labour force for the monasteries and this led to increased possibilities in agriculture. Many of the great Burgundian vineyards were originally planted by monks. We find Cistercian monasteries engaged in improved animal husbandry, and they tended to use the horse rather than oxen for ploughing, thus increasing the amount of usable land. Some monasteries had fish hatcheries along the great rivers. Improved sanitation in the monasteries, brought about by diverting streams and altering water courses, led to improved health and a better standard of living.

Observance was obviously important and this was ensured by the work of the third Abbot of Cîteaux, St Stephen Harding. His *Charter of Charity* set out the bond between monasteries and put the responsibility for the observance on the Abbot. It instituted regular visitations by the Abbot of the founding monastery and perhaps most important of all, imposed a General Chapter of Abbots to be held annually at which all matters of community life were to be discussed and regulated. Each house was obliged to follow the same customs and lifestyle. While this worked well in Europe, the spread of the Order outside Europe and North America, mainly in the past century, has led to changes. It is now up to each house to decide its own lifestyle within the limits of certain general principles.

By the middle of the 13th century, the Order had over 700 houses, spread all over Europe. Some monasteries of Benedictine nuns accepted the Cistercian Usages early on, and were recognised by the General Chapter as belonging to the Order. These continued to flourish and increase in number, as did the monasteries of men. During the following centuries there was a fall-off in numbers of men and women entering the communities and by the time of the Reformation, the Order had split into Congregations, organised more or less on language or national groupings.

Later Reforms

A number of reformers emerged and during the 17th century the most powerful and persuasive of these was the Abbot of the Abbey of La Grande Trappe in France — Armand Jean de Rancé. His reform stressed silence and abstinence, and generally embraced a very austere form of life. Many of the monasteries disagreed with de Rancé's reforms, and what become known as "The War of the Observances" took place. This led to a situation of long-standing disagreement among the monasteries, and to regrettable alienation between them. Those who followed the Reform of de Rancé came to be known as Trappists and the name has remained.

This division remained in the Order until a General Chapter of all the monasteries took place under the pontificate of Leo XIII in 1892, when it was agreed to form two separate groupings. These were OCist (Cistercians) and OCSO (Strict Observance — still popularly called Trappists). Each of these groups operates as a separate religious Order, with the Cistercians tending more towards education and pastoral work, while the Trappists remain committed to separation from society in so far as that is possible in today's world.

The Fathers of the Order

The period 1098 to 1200 must be regarded as the Golden Age of the Order. During this time a number of writers emerged who have left an indelible impression on the spirituality of the Cistercians. The following pages describes these writers and their work.

St Bernard of Clairvaux

Bernard entered the newly founded Cîteaux, then struggling with few novices, in the year 1113, accompanied by 30 companions, many of them his own relatives. Two years later, he was sent to found the Abbey of Clairvaux (also in Burgundy) and remained as its Abbot until his death in 1153. He had an extraordinarily active career in the service of the Church. He preached the Second Crusade, and was in constant demand as a mediator and peacemaker across Europe. He also had a huge literary output. He wrote a *Treatise on Spirituality* for one of his monks who had been elected Pope Eugene III, a *Treatise on Loving God*, and another on *The Degrees of Humility and Pride*. This latter was based on the model he found in the *Rule of St Benedict*.

Bernard's sermons are among the most readable and the richest of his works. Sermons for the feasts and seasons of the year, on the Virgin Mother, and particularly those on the *Song of Songs*, are a mine of Cistercian spirituality. In the latter, we have a total of 85 sermons based on the *Song of Songs*, and using its imagery to describe the progress of the spiritual life. These sermons, which were written between 1135 and the year of his death in 1153, reflect his most mature spirituality and are among the greatest examples of mediaeval mysticism. They exercised a huge influence on the Order and are widely available today in English. Added to Bernard's sermons and treatises are his letters, now available in a critical edition and translated.

Bernard's conviction is that although we are weak and prone to sin, we are also created in the image and likeness of God and hence we have from creation a tendency towards God. He is therefore optimistic about salvation and about the power of God's grace in human nature, and this is one of the most attractive traits in his writings.

St Aelred of Rievaulx

Aelred had grown up at the Scottish court and entered the monastery of Rievaulx in Yorkshire about 1134. Eventually he became Abbot and at the suggestion of St Bernard wrote his most important work, *The Mirror of Charity*, a treatise on the spiritual life. We know a great deal about Aelred from his Life, written by one of his monks after his death. It is clear that Aelred was a man of outstanding affective gifts and was much loved by his monks. He wrote a treatise on *Christian Friendship*, and his devotion to the child Jesus is clear from his meditations *On Jesus at the Age of Twelve*. But he was also firm as Abbot and showed this in his government of Rievaulx.

Two other major writers must be mentioned – Guerric of Igny and William of St Thierry. With Bernard and Aelred, these make up "The Four Evangelists" of the Cistercian Golden Age.

Guerric of Igny

Guerric of Igny was a native of Tournai and he taught there. He lived a solitary life until he visited Clairvaux in the 1120s and Bernard advised him to join the community. He did so and in 1138 went as Abbot to the monastery of Igny. He wrote over 50 sermons for the liturgical year. These are marked by gentleness and a rich devotion to the persons of Jesus Christ and Mary. He writes movingly about the spiritual maternity of Mary for every Christian, and he helped to sow the seeds of the strong devotion to the Mother of God in Cistercian spirituality. Like St Bernard, he sees the Liturgy as mirroring not only the mysteries of Jesus Christ, but also our own lives as these are touched by the saving grace of Jesus.

William of St Thierry

William of St Thierry is the fourth important figure in early Cistercian spirituality. William was Abbot of the Benedictine monastery of St Thierry and a lifelong friend of Bernard. He wanted to join Clairvaux, but Bernard was unwilling to agree to this. In 1135, William resigned his abbacy and joined the recently founded Cistercian monastery of Signy. He wrote the Life of St Bernard after the latter's death and like his friend he produced a commentary on the *Song of Songs*. His writings have a more intellectual tone than those of the other Cistercian Fathers, as William had been a student of the works of St Augustine. His treatise on *The Nature and Dignity of Love* is rather less optimistic than Bernard's approach, in that he stresses that through sin we have lost the image of God. We regain it by accepting the love of Christ for us, which gradually brings peace to the soul. William's *Golden Epistle to the Carthusians of Mont Dieu* is his finest and most contemplative work.

There were other Cistercian writers of the period. Clairvaux itself produced a number of monks who wrote in the tradition of Bernard. In England we have Baldwin of Ford, John of Ford and Gilbert of Hoyland. John of Ford continued Bernard's *Sermons on the Song of Songs* when Bernard died without finishing the series. There were still others but we have indicated enough to show that the determination of the early Cistercians to live "far from the haunts of men" and to stress poverty and simplicity of life did not detract from their output of spiritual writings.

Among the Cistercian nuns the mystical writings of "The Two Gertrudes" — Gertrude of Helfta and Gertrude of Hackeborn — must be mentioned, along with those of Mechtilde of Magdebourg. The tender affection of these saints for the person of Jesus, and the joy of their mystical experiences, helped to form the mediaeval mystical tradition which enriched the entire church.

Cistercian Spirituality Today

The Divine Office

The *Rule of St Benedict* remains the fundamental inspiration of Cistercian life. The first Fathers of the Cistercians wanted to get back to the literal interpretation of the *Rule* but as history shows they were ready to modify it and to add to it as necessary for their own time. The most evident example of this is the institution of the Lay Brothers. Benedict's teaching on the spiritual life is based on Scripture, and that comes to the monk in the daily repetition of the Divine Office. Benedict says quite simply that "nothing in the life of the monk is to be preferred to the Work of God". The Work of God is his name for the Divine Office.

The Office is now in the vernacular and while the Cistercians have never taken up the practice of the midnight office, as some other contemplative institutes do, they rise early. It is for each monastery to decide on the hour of rising, but the first office of the day (called *Vigils*) must be truly nocturnal prayer. This sets the tone of Cistercian spirituality. The monk is one who keeps vigil — he waits for the coming of the Lord. This "waiting" is done at night to underline that it is often in the hours of darkness (when it is least expected) that the Lord comes, and we know not the day nor the hour of his coming. The darkness here means not only the hours of night but the dark passages of life when all seems hopeless, and it is then the Lord comes. It is important that the church wait expectantly for his coming. She does this in the persons of the monks who keep vigil. Thus the monk's eyes are on God, and right through his life he is expectantly waiting.

The Office of Vigils begins with Psalm 94 and the repeated response to the verses which are recited solo at the beginning of each day is, "Today if you shall hear his voice, do not harden your hearts". Thus, Vigils teaches us to live in the present moment — today is all we have. Yesterday is gone for good or evil; we do not know if we shall see tomorrow. Now today — on this day which is ours by the gift of God — we will hear his voice as he calls us to come to him and to listen.

The use of the *Psalms* in the vernacular has made a great difference to the monks. The familiarity of the monk with the words of the Psalms tends to form his spiritual outlook and to confirm him in hope. Like the People of God waiting expectantly for their release from slavery and oppression, so the Church in the person of the monk waits for release from the slavery of sin and the oppression of his own selfishness. The first prayer of the day is an expression of hope that today will be the day of Redemption, what the New Testament calls "the day of Christ Jesus". The choice is always between the hardness of heart that leaves one deaf to God's voice and the opening of one's heart to hear the gentle whisper of the Spirit of God. Many of the psalms, particularly the psalms of suffering such as 21, 68 or 101, are really Passion Psalms. They speak of more than individual suffering. Only Jesus Christ the Saviour, who took the pain of the world on himself at Calvary, fulfils the words of these Psalms. So the monk learns to say these in the person of Christ, and they thus speak more of the Gospels and the Passion narratives than of the Old Testament and the period in which they were composed.

The Wider Liturgy

The liturgy shapes the day of the monk as he gathers with his brethren to pray in the Church. The Office is always the prayer of the Church. It is more than the prayer of any individual. But the monk finds himself in

the recurring cycle of the yearly feasts and seasons.
These reflect his own life. Advent sums up for him the
quality that St Benedict asks first of all of the aspiring
monk, "That he do truly seek God". So it puts the question to him: Are you really seeking God or have you
given up on that and are now seeking your own comfort
and ease and so growing in selfishness rather than in
finding God? Can you really say with St Bernard in the
Song of Songs, "I have sought him whom my soul loves
. . . "? Christmas brings him to Bethlehem where there
was no room in the inn — what about the inn of his
heart and life? Then Lent comes to remind him of the
need for penance and an asceticism that is real and
transforming. That brings him to what the Rule calls
"Holy Easter" — which should be a time of true Resurrection from the dead past of his sins to new Life in the
Risen Christ. The yearly Liturgical Cycle mirrors the life
of the monk and, if he will allow it, brings him face to
face with himself and with the demands of his vocation.
It was said that St Bernard used to ask himself, "My
friend, for what have you come here?" remembering
that the words were first used by Jesus to Judas in the
Garden just before the betrayal. The Liturgy asks the
same question of the monk with every changing season
and feast day.

The daily celebration of the *Eucharist* is the centre
of the monk's spirituality, for here he has the Word of
God leading into the Divine Ritual in which he fulfils
the only action about which Jesus the Saviour said, "Do
this in memory of me". This memory is not a mere re-

calling of the past and of what happened at the Last Supper. It is happening now and is being transformed by sharing in it. Day in, day out, of course, like any repeated human action, it can become routine and dead — but the monk cannot allow this to happen or his whole life and motivation will die also. So he needs prayer outside the Sacramental action and he needs to interiorise the Word of God.

Lectio Divina

For the monk, ruminating on the Word of God is not something different to prayer. One slips into the other, as the prayer of the monk is essentially based on the reading of the Bible. *Lectio Divina* has become popular in the past few years, so it is not necessary to explain it at length. It consists essentially in reading a passage of the Gospel, then re-reading it, and then allowing it to penetrate one's heart and mind. All the while one is open to hearing it as a New Word addressed to oneself for the first time. As the Epistle to the Hebrews says:

> *The word of God is alive and active, and it cuts more finely than any two edged sword, and can penetrate to the utmost depths of the self, where emotions and deepest feelings lie buried (cf Hebrews 4:12 seq).*

Years of *Lectio Divina* (not to be identified with Spiritual Reading, in which one seeks knowledge of the spiritual way) familiarises the monk with the Bible, particularly the revelation of God's love for us in Jesus

Christ, and this becomes his prayer, his contemplation, and his strength for the life to which he believes he has been called.

Asceticism

It is clear from the tradition that the lives of monks have always been ascetical, marked by a certain austerity of conduct and seriousness of intent. When speaking of Lent, St Benedict says that the whole life of the monk should have a Lenten character. But he goes to say that not many have the strength for this, so that during the season of Lent, the monk's life should be markedly penitential.

One would expect that a large part of this austerity or ascetical dimension of life will be found in the practice of the vows of religion. However, monks do not take the usual three vows of poverty, chastity and obedience, whereby the religious renounces possessions, marriage, and doing what one wants oneself. Monks instead take vows of Obedience, Stability and Conversion of life.

Obedience to an Abbot can mean that the monk never gets the job in the monastery that he thinks would best befit his talents and gifts. Quite apart from ambition (which St Bernard notes is the last of the passions to die) he can find himself appointed to offices which would not be his first or even second choice. Unless the monk would find it quite beyond his ability or strength, he should simply take it and get on with it as best he may. This can mean a lot of self-sacrifice. A cheerful readiness to fit in with the needs of the community is a very desirable quality in a monk. Clearly it has wider implications in that it involves a constant renunciation of what he wants for himself. Handled rightly, this experience can become a refining fire for the soul and the personality, which will lead to great spiritual growth. If it is not handled rightly, it will almost certainly lead to bitterness, complaints and an unhealthy introversion. Ideally, obedience should lead to a collaborative effort on the part of the Abbot and the monk to find God's will, which is always the good of the neighbour, in the matter.

The monk's second vow is *Stability* to the monastery/ community of his profession. He can expect in the normal course of events to spend all his life here in this monastery with these men. Except in rare and special cases, he will not be sent to another abbey. One of the traditional descriptions of the monk is that he be "a lover of the brethren and of the place". This is the ideal behind stability. We live in a world of movement. We can go around the world not in the 80 days of Jules Verne's adventure story but in a few hours, and we can go round it in thought and imagination in an instant. We are constantly bombarded with images and ideas. We need to sit still and not only accept our limitations and our smallness, but be aware that it is in stillness and quiet that we hear the gentle wind of the Spirit. We need to realise that our lives take on importance only when they are filled with God and his spirit. Achievement and success are drugs, and generally in community life they are reduced to their correct proportions. If

we live as hermits, we have no one with whom to practise charity. But more than that, it is only the rare soul
who can learn to know himself without the daily interaction that goes on all the time in a community. Stability anchors the monk to the place, and to these men
with whom he lives. He can dream of a practice of charity that might take place elsewhere, while neglecting the
people with whom he lives and interacts every day. Not
only is this the day of salvation but it is here in this
place, ordinary, boring at times maybe, but still his
home, that the spiritual combat is fought and the two
commandments of Jesus applied.

The monk's third vow is *Conversion*. The Latin
phrase is *Conversio Morum,* and this has been vari-
ously translated by commentators on the *Rule of Benedict*. The best and in the end the most accurate seems to
be simply Conversion of Life. This is not just a matter of
telling myself day after day that I am getting better. On
the contrary, it means coming to true self-knowledge,
for without knowledge of self (which is a rare commod-
ity even among sincere people) one will not come to
knowledge of God. Neither does a vow of conversion
mean that I spend time "reflecting on my sins". This
rarely does people much good and tends only to depress
them. God is my salvation and if my strength is in Him,
then I shall not fail and no one or nothing can take Him
from me. As Paul says, "Nothing in all creation can
separate us from the love of God in Christ Jesus our
Lord". That is the meaning of conversion — a commit-

ment to that love which will overcome all obstacles, and most of all those I find in myself.

Silence

We must say something about silence, which assumed an importance in the history of the Cistercians which many feel was exaggerated. It received such emphasis in the Trappist reform that it became synonymous with "Trappist". The Trappists were the Silent Order, and many believed they even took a vow of silence, which was never the case. But it was true that they never spoke to each other or did so only with permission from the Abbot, and all necessary communication was by means of a language of hand signs.

In the Reforms that followed the Second Vatican Council, these signs were abandoned and any necessary communication is by speech. But it is clear that silence is a most important element of the monk's life. If he is constantly chattering, he will never grow spiritually. If he spends his time reading the newspapers and listening to radio, his mind will be filled with the doings of society, most often those which are least likely to build up a solid faith and an awareness of the presence of God in daily life. Silence is a serious ascetical practice and a monastery should be redolent of silence. One expects a monastic community to be composed of serious-minded men, not unduly solemn or introverted, neither gloomy nor self-absorbed, but cheerful and healthily concerned for others, while preserving a spirit of silence that can be filled with God.

Manual Work

The early Cistercians believed strongly that monks should live by the labour of their hands, and the ideal remains true to this day. Work is an important element of life, not merely of monastic life. Without it we are living on the work of others, and we are in danger of a life of idleness. Work is healing in that it can take us out of ourselves and often enough it is the solace of those who are lonely, depressed or out of sorts. Work is essential for good mental and psychological health.

But more than that is the fact that monasteries do not live on alms. Monks work for their living and in the modern world this has led to considerable diversification. Formerly it was taken for granted that the monasteries live by farming and the rearing of cattle. This was even stated in the *Constitutions*. With the developments in agriculture in the modern world, particularly during the last half century, this is becoming less feasible as communities grow older, men and women live longer, and the economics of farming have changed drastically. Nowadays, monasteries produce and market a range of saleable goods — wine and beer, honey and jam and jellies, cheese and cakes and mail order Eucharist Bread, cards and printed matter, computer services and vegetables and milk. Monks live by their own work, and there is work for everyone in the monastery.

Hospitality

Every monastery has a building for the reception of guests. Again to quote St Benedict: "Guests are never

wanting in a monastery . . . and they are to be received
as Christ himself". Monks regard the exercise of the
Christian virtue of hospitality as important. Monasteries
provide a place of refuge, a haven of quiet and of prayer,
where people can come and rest, aside from the turmoil
of the world and the ever-increasing pressures of daily
life. Monasteries do not provide holiday facilities but
places of prayer and recollection. The guests are encouraged to join in the daily Offices, and to share in the daily
Community Eucharist with the monks. But on the
whole, guests tend to be left on their own, and as the
monasteries are not organised like retreat houses, each
one can find their own level of prayer and quiet, and just
soak in the peace and rest that comes with a few days'
withdrawal from the busyness of life.

Devotion to the Blessed Virgin Mary

We have already spoken of the strong current of sincere
devotion to the Mother of Jesus which runs through the
writings of the early Cistercian Fathers. It would be a
mistake to think that this is merely a matter of singing
the praises of Mary. As well as doing that, Bernard pro-
poses her as a model for the Christian. The following is
from a *Sermon for the Birthday of the Blessed Virgin.*
He has spoken of her as a conduit bringing the waters of
the well of life to us. He continues:

> But how could this conduit reach above the
> heavens to the well of living water? How do you
> think, except by the fervour of her devotion, the
> vehemence of her longings and the purity of her

> *prayers. . . . How did she reach up to the*
> *inaccessible majesty of God except by knocking,*
> *asking, seeking?*

Clearly this is as much about prayer as about the Virgin Mary, and Bernard is implicitly proposing her as a model for the Christian at prayer.

5

DOMINICAN SPIRITUALITY

Aidan Nichols, OP

The Church is "surrounded with variety" (Psalm 44, 10). *Circumdata varietate*: that, at any rate, is how the Latin Bible translates the Hebrew of the Psalter in a text that St Thomas Aquinas regarded as crucial for understanding why there are so many kinds of religious family within the one body of Christ.[1]

Who was St Dominic?

Though Thomas is the most important spiritual figure the Dominicans have produced, he would have considered himself a son of St Dominic.[2] To understand the spirituality of the Order of Preachers, we have to go back to their common father.

In 1198, Domingo de Guzman, the son of a Castilian squire, left his university city, Palencia, where his parents had sent him to study the arts, and later theology. Perhaps owing to his generosity in selling his books and setting up an almonry to help the poor during a famine, he had caught the eye of the bishop of Osma, Martin Bazan. Bishop Martin invited Dominic to join the community of regular canons attached to the cathedral there. These canons wore a white habit, a sign that they were clerics who had accepted strict ascetic customs to regulate a common life modelled on that of the apostles after the Resurrection. Dominic began to live with very great spiritual fervour.

In 1203, Dominic accompanied Martin's successor, Diego de Acebes, on a diplomatic visit to Denmark in the service of the King of Castile. On their way through southern France they encountered members of the "anti-church" of the Catharists: supporters of a wildly heretical view of Christianity, who believed in a dual origin for the world with a good principle for spirit, an evil one for matter. When the Pope, Innocent III, refused Bishop Diego permission to become a missionary among the pagan Tartars, he turned his attention to this need for Catholic evangelism nearer home. Realising that the gracious lifestyle of the Abbot of Cîteaux and other Cistercian legates, papally entrusted with this mission, compared unfavourably in people's eyes with the simple ways of the Catharist preachers, Diego proposed a new form of preaching, to be lived out in evangelical poverty. His brother bishop in Toulouse, Fulk, himself a Cistercian, fully supported the idea, and so Diego seconded Dominic and some other canons of Osma for the "holy preaching" in the heartlands of Catharism. The next years would be occupied by preaching tours, public debates and — not least — the establishment of a monastery of nuns where converts among the educated women members of the sect could lead a religious life, and help others like themselves. A little house for the preachers was attached thereto.

In 1215 Dominic and his co-workers were given a new home in Toulouse itself and authority from the bishop to assist him in all forms of doctrinal ministry. Getting preaching assistance for bishops had been a major preoccupation of the Third Lateran Council in 1179. The situation would be no different at the Fourth Lateran Council of 1215, which Fulk and Dominic attended. There Innocent III suggested that the preachers should go on to become not just a diocesan institute but an Order at the service of the universal Church. Dominic at once began to organise, taking as his guide the *Rule of St Augustine* and the *Premonstratensian Book of Customs* with which he was evidently already familiar. Bishop Fulk gave the new preaching canons their first church, St Romain at Toulouse, and two others in the diocese to staff when human resources made it possible. Realising the importance of the best theological education possible, Dominic sent his brethren to school, first at Toulouse, and then to the premier university of the Latin West, Paris.

In 1218 a new Pope, Honorius III, wrote the first of a series of bulls recommending Dominic's preachers to all the bishops of the Church. It marks the earliest appearance of the phrase "Order of Preachers". In a pardonable exaggeration:

> *. . . before Dominic's death, Honorius had in ef-*
> *fect reversed the decree of Lateran IV: instead*
> *of urging the bishops to seek the help of auxil-*
> *iary preachers, he was summoning the bishops*
> *to assist the Order of Preachers.*[3]

There began a whole series of foundations, notably in university and cathedral cities in Italy and Spain. Personally, however, Dominic never abandoned his original methods of itinerant preaching, combined with the creation or consolidation of houses of contemplative women to act as centres of intercession and sisterly support.

In 1220 he brought the brethren together in their first General Chapter at Bologna, where the essential legal framework of the Order was put in place. It consisted of elective democracy at all levels, from the priory, through the Province — the network of priories in a given country or region — to the Order as a whole. At each level, a chapter assisted the superior, whether conventual prior, provincial prior or Master (who, for his lifetime, was Dominic himself). Each community was to have a *doctor*, a lecturer in theology, in residence, and to be a place of theological study and teaching.

In 1221 a second General Chapter determined on the expansion of the Order to England, Poland, Hungary and (possibly) Greece. On the feast of the Transfiguration, 6 August, that year, Dominic died at Bologna in the odour of sanctity. In 1233 his remains were translated to a more fitting tomb in the priory that now bears his name, the "patriarchal convent". Pope Gregory IX canonised him in 1234, by which date the Dominicans were already involved in missions to pagans and Muslims, and efforts to bring back separated Eastern Christians into unity with Rome.

So much for the history, which shows us the original charisma of St Dominic taking flesh in a corporate and therefore institutional way. What, then, is the nature of Dominican religious life, and why does its spirituality matter?

The Particular Goal of Dominican Spirituality: Preaching the Word

All Christian spirituality has the same ultimate goal, which is the perfect love of God and our neighbour on the basis of the work of Christ and after his example. The riches of grace and the variety of human temperament being what they are, this ultimate goal can take the form of more than one particular goal. The particular goal of Dominican spirituality is the preaching of the Word of God. The primitive *Constitutions* declare the Order to have been founded for "preaching and the salvation of souls"; that is, preaching and the salvation of others insofar as that can be encompassed through preaching and teaching.

Any account of Dominican spirituality must take its bearings mainly from the friars, whose brotherhood Dominic set out chiefly to form. Their preaching normally entails the priesthood, which is the ministry sacramentally ordained for the proclamation of the Word. Indeed, that preaching issues most fully in the celebra-

tion and reception of sacraments, notably the Holy
Eucharist. Some friars are "co-operator" brothers, who,
typically, look after the material care of the houses of
the Order, in this way assisting its preaching. Dominican cloistered nuns, who, as we have seen, were part of
Dominic's project from the beginning, also "preach" by
the testimony of the enclosed contemplative life. Their
way of life carries an intimate relation to that of the
brethren, for the latter are expected to exercise their
preaching ministry by an overflow of contemplation. It
is intended that a common, liturgical, studious and austere life, animated by a spirituality that is strongly intellectual yet also devotional, will make this possible.

In later generations, the Dominicans also acquired
an "order of penance", the ancestor of today's "Lay Dominicans". Such layfolk are invited to make Dominican
spirituality their own — which involves them too, then,
in preaching in a wide sense: explaining the faith to
others or at least giving witness to it, according to their
possibilities. The position of the many Congregations of
Dominican sisters is less clear-cut. Often the result of
non-Dominican initiatives, they belong not to the Order
in the strict sense but to a broader "Dominican family"
or association. But *some* relation to the preaching of the
Word there must be if any group in the Church is ap-
propriately to be affiliated to the Order of Preachers.

As we have seen, St Dominic changed the canonical
life by giving it a new missionary purpose which looked
beyond the ordinary duties of the priesthood in a given
locality to doctrinal preaching in the universal Church.

In Dominic's day, the meaning of the term "apostolic life" — originally confined to a common life on the model of the Jerusalem church of the Acts — was already shifting. Even for the regular canons, whose ministry was chiefly pastoral, the preaching of the Word was treated as a distinctively apostolic task, one that continued the preaching ministry of the Twelve in Galilee, continued it (usually) for the benefit of the faithful living in the parochial jurisdiction of an abbey. But among the plethora of lay movements within or beyond the boundaries of orthodoxy at the turn of the 12th and 13th centuries, the true *vita apostolica* was a life of itinerant preaching to all and sundry, to anybody and everybody. The Dominicans combined two senses of apostolic living. By integrating the new sense of apostolic mission with the older sense of shared, apostolic community, they became in effect the first missionary order in the Church's history.

Later on, when other missionary Orders and Congregations come along, the Dominicans will remain distinctive. Not only will they retain the canonical life (that other meaning of the phrase "the apostolic life") in their priories; they will also conceive *mission* in terms of the two related titles found in the bull of confirmation of the Order by Honorius III. The first of those titles was *ordo praedicatorum,* an Order of Preachers, meaning preachers of the faith in its fundamental elements, whether to outsiders or to rudimentarily instructed believers. The second title was *ordo doctorum*, an Order of doctors or teachers to expound doctrine to Christians, whether laity or clergy, who already have more than just the basics. Even when the term *ordo doctorum* falls into disuse, the preaching will still be understood in a way that emphasises doctrine. It will be the exposition and exploration of the biblical revelation as construed by reference to the Church's rule of faith.

"Preaching" here does not mean simply preaching in church, though that is its most obvious and central example. It means any proclamation in language of the divine Word. Whatever the level of instruction involved, and this could range from basic catechesis to the most comprehensively systematic theology, it is typical of Dominican preaching that it has a doctrinal ethos or temper.

That is most obviously true of the Dominican saints who were celebrated as thinkers. We see it with Albert the Great; we see it with Thomas. But the doctrinal cast of preaching in our Order is characteristic not just of an Albert or a Thomas, theologians who were highly trained in what we should now call metaphysics, patristics and exegesis. It is also true of an unlettered lay Dominican like Catherine of Siena for whom an understanding of the Trinity, Christology, the Atonement, the mystery of the Church, was equally vital to the Christian life. As she says of herself in the opening of the *Dialogue*, "Loving, she seeks to pursue truth and clothe herself in it".[4] All three were deeply formed by doctrine in such a way that we have to speak of the *intellectual* cast of their spirituality and therefore of their holiness as well.

The Means to Preaching (1): The Common Life

In any given spirituality, the particular goal is arrived at by particular means. The first of these essential means to preaching as Dominicans see it is the common life. In *The Acts of the Apostles*, the apostolic community — that is, the original Jerusalem church after Pentecost — had lived a common life where no one called anything his own. It was a life centring on the preaching of the Word of God, the Breaking of Bread (an ancient name for the Holy Eucharist), and "the prayers" — doubtless Christianised forms of Jewish prayer hours which anticipated the later Church's "Divine Office". This was in essence the same life lived centuries later by "canons regular" — clerics who lived a common life with the moderate asceticism recommended by Church canons, undertook the solemn — that is the sung — celebration of the daily services, and took for their rule of life one or more of the various documents produced for this purpose from the patristic period onwards. Of these documents, the *Rule of Augustine* had emerged by the early 11th century as incomparably the chief. From the point of view of common life, Dominican life is a subset of Augustinian life. The first of the means to the goal of Dominican spirituality concerns this kind of "apostolic" living.

The Rule declares that the first reason the members of a *monasterium* are gathered into one is to live unanimously in the house, having one soul and one heart intent upon God. For the author of Acts, and not only in his account of the Jerusalem church, unanimity is a hallmark of the community that carries the Gospel.

It is of course unanimity in what concerns Christian revelation — not on a host of civil matters where a degree of variability in judgement is a precondition of a healthy public opinion. Obedience to the Word of God means the making of a common mind, and, something even more difficult given the vagaries of human temperament, a common heart. A common mind and heart are possible if they are part and parcel of a spiritual moving together towards God, something conveyed with beautiful brevity by Augustine when he adds that the one mind and one heart concerned are that of people living, as he puts it, *in Deum*, that is, "intent upon God".

In a somewhat fractured Catholic Church, the attempt to live unanimously is an important witness. As a reminiscence, perhaps of the incarnational emphasis of Dominic's preaching which, over against the Cathars, was centred on the Word made *flesh*, the primitive Dominican *Constitutions* insisted that this unity should not only be internal but external. It should be *embodied*.

> *It is right that, as we live under one Rule and by the vow of a single profession, so uniformity of observance should be found in our Order so that the unity kept in our hearts may be fostered and represented by the exterior uniformity kept in our customs.*[5]

One might ask, though, what has this to do with holiness and therefore spirituality? As a variety of comments scattered through St Augustine's corpus of writing makes clear, it has a great deal to do with holiness, especially by way of the concept of charity.[6]

In his discourse on Psalm 132, "Behold how good and lovely it is, brothers dwelling in unity", Augustine maintains that the presence and action of the Holy Spirit become manifest as the charity that makes brotherly concord possible. And so the religious community, whose members "live in the house in unity of spirit" (see Psalm 67, 7), is a model of the Church, the Temple of God, a temple formed by the living stones of "those who are united by charity".[7] Such a community is also an image of the heavenly city. The members of that city form a community where "there is . . . a love that rejoices in a good that is at once shared by all and [yet] unchanging".[8]

Finally, this unity-in-charity reflects the life of the Trinity itself:

> *"They were of one soul and one heart towards God." Listen, brothers, and from this recognise the mystery of the Trinity.*[9]

Such concord expresses the mystery of the Church, the hope of heaven and the life of the Blessed Trinity. "I believe in . . . the holy Catholic Church". Dominican preaching of the Word is done from a life of common charity with a view to building up the Church as Christ's mystical body.

The Means to Preaching (2): The Sacred Liturgy

This life of apostolic communion is sustained by a liturgical communion, a common sharing in the mysteries of the Church. If you go to the chapter house of the canons of Osma, you can still see on the central capital of one wall a Romanesque sculpture showing the *Mandatum*, the washing of the feet of the apostles by Jesus at the Last Supper. In such houses the Mandatum was frequently re-enacted in chapter as a kind of sacramental to reinforce the Augustinian message of brotherly love. This reminds us that the spiritual life of the canons was first and foremost a liturgical life that found its sustenance in the devout celebration of the Mass and the liturgical hours. These were of course known to Augustine, but by the high mediaeval period their careful celebration had come to take on much greater prominence. St Dominic will pass onto his brethren the canon's love of the Mass and fidelity to the praying of the Divine Office wherever possible in choir, with the gestures and chant that belong to solemn celebration — even though, so as to facilitate the apostolic goal of his Order, a principle of dispensation from choir Office will be built in for when the preaching apostolate, and its immediate preparation in study, require this. So, after the common life, the liturgical life is the second building block of Dominican spirituality.

Once again it is a very desirable one for the Church today where spirituality has sometimes become disengaged from the Liturgy. Many of our contemporaries, even if more or less meeting the formal obligations of religious practice, do not expect to find spiritual nourishment in the rites of the Church — the sacraments and sacramentals, the cycle of feasts and seasons, the treasury of the missal and the liturgical hours. They look instead to other models and sources, rather sub-Christian in character — for meditation and contemplation. We can say that, to a certain degree, the Liturgy and contemplation have become separated one from another. For many people, the Liturgy has become uncontemplative and contemplation has become aliturgical. This is impossible for Dominicans who take from the canonical tradition, as embodied in St Dominic, the assumption that the two — Liturgy and contemplation — belong together. The texts of the Liturgy are the discourse of the Church as the Bride of Christ reliving salvation history and bringing before God the entire range of human needs which, for example, the Psalter, the staple of the Divine Office, contains.

What the friar studies in his cell he contemplates in the Liturgy. The great New Testament scholar Marie-Joseph Lagrange called Dominican life a "coming and going between oratory and laboratory". The truths of faith and morals we investigate by study come alive for us in choir.

The primitive *Constitutions* ask that the Office be not recited too slowly lest this harm study, but they also say it should not be recited too quickly lest this undermine devotion. This is summed up in the phrase *breviter et succincte*: "briefly and . . ." — and what? Suggestions range from "eagerly" to "strictly". Anyway

it is just as well that *breviter* is in there since Dominic
and the first brethren committed themselves not only to
the normal Office, the "Great Office", but to the daily
recitation in shifts, mostly in the Dormitory, of the Little Office of our Lady, as well as the Office of the Dead
to be recited representatively each day by four friars in
each priory. (Later it would be said by the entire community once a week.) Though these specific practices
were gradually abandoned, they draw attention to the
strongly marked Marian element in Dominican spirituality — the Order's guardianship of the Rosary is the
most obvious expression of this — and its commitment
to prayer for the departed, which carries a strong sense
of the communion of saints.

The Means to Preaching (3): Study

The adjective "intellectual" is rarely yoked together with
the nouns "spirituality" or "holiness". Perhaps in Eng-
lish-speaking countries, where intellectuals are generally believed to be an aberration, usually French, this
might be thought to be no bad thing. The fact is, however, that the life of the intellect — seeking the truth —
is part and parcel of our human make-up, from which it
follows that, in the words of the Anglican philosopher
and exegete Austin Farrer, an unintellectual salvation
means an unsaved intellect. Moreover, ideas, as they
seep down, bring enormous force to bear on people's
outlooks. One need only think of the impact of scientific
theory, especially in an area like evolution, or of a moral
theory such as Utilitarianism. Today, much of the rea-

son why people do not take the claims of revelation seriously, and so cannot grow in holiness in the way revelation as found in the life of the Church makes possible, stems from the fact that they regard Christianity, not least in its Catholic form, as inherently incredible. Many contemporary Catholics seem to think it is enough to present the Church in moral terms — as "listening", "caring" and so forth. In many contexts such virtues, however admirable, do not even begin to address the basic problem. Dominican preaching, taken in that wider sense which includes writing, lecturing, debating or just taking part in apostolically relevant conversation, has to be intellectually well prepared, no matter what the level of sophistication at which it takes place.

Hence the major role played by study in the Dominican life. "The bow is first bent in study, and then in preaching the arrow is let fly", wrote Hugh of St Cher, our greatest pre-Scholastic theologian, in the introduction to his seven-volume commentary on Scripture.[10] This is an Order where the common life and the liturgical life are at the service of a mission first to study revealed truth (and the disciplines that enable one to grasp it) and then to communicate that truth to others. As such it is both unique and specially needed in a secularised environment. The kind of holiness it espouses — an intellectual holiness of minds set aflame by truth to be in love with God — is likewise especially needed as a form of witness today when intellectuality and spirituality have fallen apart.

In principle, anything — from hummingbirds to nuclear fission — can be studied in the light of God. But
Dominican study centres on divine revelation in its
transmission through the Church. It focuses, that is, on
the sources of revelation, Scripture and Tradition, or better, Scripture read in Tradition. So the Bible, the Fathers,
and the great Doctors of the Church are its favourite sub-
jects. But just as Dominic, confronted by the Cathars,
was obliged to defend the goodness of creation, and the
identity of the God of creation with the Trinity revealed
in Christ, so Dominican study came to pay special attention to philosophy, and notably to metaphysics. Nature is
not only the fruit of the act of creation. It has also been
taken up by grace when the Word assumed our humanity
and through the sacraments, which are the continuation
of that humanity, continues to act for our redemption.
Appreciating that in studious depth is integral to Dominican spirituality too.

The Means to Preaching (4): Monastic Observance

Giving the canonical life a missionary finality was not
the only way in which Dominic changed its pattern. The
other change he made was to radicalise its asceticism.
The reformed canons regular of his period had taken
various spiritual themes and practices from the monastic tradition in one or the other of its two historic forms,
the hermit life and the life of cenobites. (By the latter is
meant monks living in community, the Cistercians be-

ing generally deemed the most admirable of these.) Dominic too plundered the Egyptians.

From the "little book" on the beginnings of the Order written by Dominic's successor as Master, Blessed Jordan of Saxony, we know that, long before he "became a Dominican", St Dominic was nourished by certain monastic themes originating outside the tradition of the canons. For example, he integrated into his spiritual outlook much of the teaching of the desert fathers — on the vices and virtues, the gift of tears, compunction and praying for sinners — as found in the *Conferences* of John Cassian, a Latin-speaking visitor to the eremitical settlements of early Christian Egypt. And in his life as a canon, Dominic made much use of such characteristically monastic practices as prolonged personal or secret prayer, notably in the form of night vigils. Dominic went so far as to advise his brethren to speak either about God or to God, a phrase he had taken, apparently, from a contemporary Rule for hermits.[11] From a text that describes his devotional habits, *The Nine Ways of Prayer*, we know that he practised *lectio Divina*, the kind of prayerful reading or mulling over of texts from the Bible recommended in Cassian and the early monastic rules. We can see the *lectio* tradition continuing in the letters of Jordan to a Dominican nun. The spiritual interpretation of Scripture in these letters closely resembles that of the best known of the Cistercian Doctors, St Bernard.

That is a significant pointer to what was happening, but pilfering from the monastic tradition so as to radi-

calise the asceticism, precisely, of the canonical life is
better exemplified in Dominic's attitude to poverty. In
part, his embracing poverty was simply a tactic, devised
to show hangers-on of the Catharist preachers that
Catholics too could do this sort of thing. More profoundly, it fitted with the kind of Order he was creating
that friars should be stripped for action, not weighed
down with impedimenta in moving from place to place,
or house to house. But such freeing from material ties
was not only to make it possible to travel light. The
early Dominicans came to envisage poverty — absolute
for individuals, relative for communities — as an intrinsic part of a consistent lifestyle. By taking over a more
austere regimen from the Cistercians via the Premonstratensians, the primitive *Constitutions* of Dominic's
Order generated a type of conventual life that was as
much monastic as it was canonical.

Where such "radicalising" is most evident is in the
great emphasis placed by the early Dominicans on the
observance of silence. *Silentium pater praedicatorum*
— "silence is the father of preachers". So the maxim had
it. When Bede Jarrett, the greatest provincial prior the
English Dominicans have produced, was writing to the
Province for the 700th anniversary of St Dominic's
death in 1921, he said:

> *Our religious life should above all centre upon*
> *(1) the punctual discipline of community life, (2)*
> *the law of silence, (3) the [sic] devout attention*
> *to the Divine Office.*[12]

To regard silence as, in this way, equivalent in importance to the common life and the liturgical life goes beyond the canonical in the direction of the monastic tradition. But it also fits very well with an Order whose mission places such a great premium on study.

If we leave aside the Dominican martyrs of various places and periods, the majority of the saints and blesseds of the Order derive from movements of strict observance. In part, Observantine movements were concerned with things that would be — by and large — taken for granted among the Friars Preachers today: the common purse, not private incomes; serious not perfunctory study; not abusing the principle of dispensation by granting a general leave of absence from choir to favoured individuals like masters in theology. But such movements were also concerned with mortification, the practice of severe asceticism, as if all the walking on unmade roads to be done on preaching assignments were not enough. Under this rubric, strict observance has meant a variety of things both for the friars and the nuns — not just the cultivation of silence but also the chapter of faults for offences against fraternal charity and the discipline of the house, the breaking of sleep for the night office, penitential fasting (interpreted more severely than in the general law of the Church) and perpetual abstinence from meat, not to mention the prohibition of the wearing of non-woollen garments next to the skin. In monasticism proper such practices, when found, are prized as aids to inner conversion primarily. In the Dominican context, they have a somewhat differ-

ent meaning. As explained by the most famous pro-
tagonist of strict or primitive observance in modern
times, the mid-to-late 19th-century Master of the Order,
Vincent Jandel, observances are a "safeguard of study
and zeal".[13] It is possible for Dominican study to become that of inquisitive people with time on their
hands, in which case its supernatural basis and orientation to the missionary apostolate can be lost. And if
study, or the intensive intellectual preparation of
preaching activity, is intrinsic to distinctively Dominican holiness, then — should we allow some merit to
Jandel's argument — the use of silence and other forms
of austerity will be instrumentally intrinsic to it too. In
the Constitutions of the enclosed Dominican nuns,
there is an echo of this idea that observances concern
mission when observance is described as a way of sharing in the mystery of redemption not only for the nuns
themselves but also for the sake of the world.[14]

The stamp of austerity St Dominic wanted his Order
to have can be a counter-cultural sign. Austerity is a
counter-cultural sign insofar as it involves a radical dis-
engagement from consumerism and hedonism. While
all matter is good and so is pleasure as the bloom on
actions that are congruent with our nature, the way
consumerism and hedonism treat matter and pleasure
in modern Western culture must surely be called obstacles to holiness for those who are most taken by them.

A Thomist Finale

Lastly, Dominican spirituality matters to the Church because in their classical theologian, St Thomas, and the writers of his school, Dominicans have a very good teaching about what holiness is. They have an excellent story about what makes spirituality tick in St Thomas's account of the virtues — natural and supernatural — and those Gifts of the Holy Spirit which perfect the operation of the virtues by making us more readily responsive to divine leading. It is a story that enables us to grasp the principles that underlie growth in holiness, including the development of the contemplative awareness that, in some form of other, accompanies such growth.[15] It shows us how wonderfully fitting to our humanity grace is, for we have a natural desire for beatitude to which only God can answer.

With St Thomas, Dominican writers on prayer and mysticism customarily emphasise the theological virtue of faith. When the word "theological" qualifies "virtue" here it tells us that the capacity in question comes from God and orients us to God. Faith affords us direct contact with the divine reality. Christian mysticism is simply the translation into experience of what faith-contact already is. The gift of supernatural Wisdom sensitises us to the mystery of God in his self-revelation. It gives us a taste of his beatifying beauty.

Dominican spirituality, then, not only puts faith to good use by biblical and doctrinal study but seeks the gift of supernatural Wisdom from the Holy Spirit, as well as the generosity to pass on the fruits of contem-

plation to others. People — especially laywomen and
nuns — with very different calls than this to the ascetical and mystical life (notably, strongly affective calls
attracting them to the Passion of Christ) have often
been drawn to the Order of Preachers, feeling the need
for a context that was intellectually solid yet spiritually
supernatural. That is how such figures as St Catherine
dei Ricci or St Rose of Lima entered our ambit. They
help the practitioners of this fundamentally intellectual-
ist spirituality to recover some of Dominic's personal
spirit of mortification and warmth of devotional prayer,
both of which went far beyond what the *Constitutions*
of his Order have ever proposed.

Notes

---

[1]   Thomas Aquinas, *Summa theologiae* IIa. IIae, q. 188, a.
      1, sed contra.

[2]   J.P. Torrell, OP (1996), *Saint Thomas d'Aquin, maître
      spirituel*, Fribourg: Editions Universitaires de Fribourg.

[3]   S. Tugwell, OP (2001), *Saint Dominic and the Order of
      Preachers*, Dublin: Dominican Publications, p. 27.

[4]   Catherine of Siena (1980), *The Dialogue*, Translation and
      Introduction by Susan Noffke, OP, London: SPCK, p. 25.

[5]   A.H. Thomas, OP (ed.) (1965), *De oudste Constituties van
      de Dominicanen*, Louvain: Leuvense Universitaire Uit-
      gaven, , p. 311.

[6]   See the essays in *La Charité et l'unité. Une clé pour en-
      trer dans la théologie de saint Augustin*, Paris: Mame,
      1993.

[7]   Augustine, *Sermon* 336, 1.

[8]   Idem., *The City of God,* XV. 3.

[9]   Idem., *Tractates on the Gospel of John*, 39, 5.

[10] Hugh of Saint-Cher, *Opera omnia in universum vetus et novum testamentum*, I. 13.

[11] *Sententiae Sancti Stephani* for which see the *Patrologia Latina*, volume 204, at column 1102.

[12] B. Bailey, A. Bellenger, S. Tugwell (eds.) (1989), *Letters of Bede Jarrett*, Bath: Downside Abbey, and Oxford: Blackfriars Publications, p. 49.

[13] Letter to Pio Nono, cited in R. Devas, OP (1913), *The Dominican Revival in the Nineteenth Century,* London: Burns and Oates, p. 53.

[14] *Liber Constitutionum Monalium*, 35, 1–3.

[15] A. Gardeil, OP (1952), *The Gifts of the Holy Ghost in the Dominican Saints,* Milwaukee: Herder; M.M. Philipon, OP (1959), "Les dons du saint-Esprit chez saint Thomas d'Aquin", *Revue Thomiste*, 59, pp. 451–483.

6

FRANCISCAN SPIRITUALITY

Francis Cotter, OFM

Introduction

"Spirituality is theology walking!" Spirituality is what we do because of what we say we believe. An authentic spirituality incarnates our beliefs. Franciscan spirituality flows from the particular vision of God and the Christian life granted to Francis of Assisi, a vision lived out radically and joyfully by the saint and his companions. In the long history of the Franciscan movement many saints, mystics and theologians have enriched the tradition. But the story and the writings of Francis serve as *the* privileged witnesses to the founding grace, and are the sources used in this reflection.

Born in the city of Assisi in central Italy in 1182, Francis was the son of a wealthy cloth merchant and worked in the family business. He was a carefree and popular young man, but a restlessness made Francis seek more from life. He failed in his attempt to achieve glory as a soldier. After a period of imprisonment and illness, he was drawn to prayer and solitude. Following an encounter with lepers, he abandoned his former life. For two years he lived as a hermit, serving the lepers and rebuilding ruined churches around Assisi. After hearing the Gospel account of the sending out of the disciples, he began to preach simply, calling people to repentance and a return to God's love. It was then that others joined him, striving to live the Gospel without compromise and in poverty and simplicity. Verbal approval for this new way of life was given by Pope Innocent III in 1210. Within ten years, there were thousands of Friars Minor spreading throughout Europe. Clare di Favarone, a young noble woman, was also inspired by Francis to follow the poor Christ. This was the beginning of the Poor Sisters, later the Poor Clares. Many lay men and women were attracted by the friars' radical living of the Christian life. To them Francis gave guidance, and, in time, the Franciscan Third Order developed. In 1224 Francis received the stigmata on Mount La Verna. Two years later, he died at Assisi renowned as the *Poverello,* the little poor one, the Lord's true disciple.

The Fullness of All Good

Traditionally, Franciscan spirituality has been seen as Christocentric with emphasis on "the crib, the Cross and the cup" (of the Eucharist). But Francis's view of the Christian life is wider and deeper than what is usually understood. He presents a profound Trinitarian vision that delights in our intimate relationship with the Father, Son and Holy Spirit. At the heart of Franciscan spirituality is a joyous celebration of the Fatherhood of God. Francis's father, in a last attempt to turn his son from the path he was taking, brought him before the Bishop of Assisi to demand restitution for the cloth Francis had sold to repair the little church of San Damiano. Standing naked before the bishop and townspeople, Francis said, as he laid his clothes at his father's feet:

> *From now on I will say freely: "Our Father who art in heaven", and not "My father, Pietro di Bernadone".*[1]

With this dramatic gesture, Francis abandons himself into God's care, totally dependent on him. He stood before God naked, little, poor and with childlike confidence and daring. Living as the Father's child, Francis discovers that God indeed can be trusted. All is mercy and gift! Franciscan joy flows from the truth that grace abides at the centre of all. Secure in God's loving providence, Francis can pray:

> *You are security . . . You are the protector, You are our guardian and defender, You are strength; You are refreshment.*[2]

But Francis does not try to domesticate or tame God. God is always "most high, all powerful, admirable and glorious, who alone is holy, praiseworthy and blessed".[3] We cannot rejoice fully in the immanence of God if we have not first glimpsed His absolute transcendence. Gratitude and praise before God's unspeakable goodness to His creatures is at the core of the Franciscan charism. Thanksgiving is not simply a virtue among others but forms the very climate in which we should live. Francis experiences God as goodness. It is a recurring refrain throughout his life. God is "the Fullness of Good, all good, every good, the true and supreme good, Who alone is Good."[4] Francis is intoxicated with the pure love of God revealed in our creation and redemption. He seeks to draw us into his passion and enthusiasm for God. He sees a kind of hedonism or pleasure seeking in the spiritual life. But it is the seeking for pleasure in which the sole object is God himself. For Francis, God is "lovable, delectable and totally desirable above all else."[5] Therefore the call is to "love, honour, adore, serve, praise and bless, glorify and exalt, magnify and give thanks to the most high and supreme eternal God".[6]

So the "Spirit of prayer and devotion" must have priority in our lives and "all other things of our earthly existence must contribute" to it.[7] In fact, it is not generally know that the eremitical life, with the Franciscan dimension of fraternity included, has been an aspect of the vision from the beginning. Francis himself, while on fire with the desire to invite people to a deeper knowledge and love of God, spent lengthy periods in various hermitages. He even wrote a little rule for those who wish to live as hermits for a time and, as he put it, quoting Christ, "seek first of all the kingdom of God and His justice [Matthew 6:33]."[8] While this element of the life was never lost, it has been revitalised in recent decades with the establishment of more hermitages of three or four Franciscans devoting themselves to contemplation. In a passage remarkable for its energy, Francis expands on the Scriptures (see Mark 12:30) in insisting on a total gift of ourselves to God:

> *Let us love the Lord God with all our heart, all our soul, with all our mind and all our strength and with fortitude and with total understanding, with all of our powers, with every effort, every affection, every emotion, every desire, and every wish. He has given and gives to each one of us our whole body, our whole soul, and our whole life. He created us and redeemed us, and will save us by His mercy alone.*[9]

According to the Holy Gospel

Francis knows that the way of life which he followed and proposed to others can always only be a response to the mystery of love that is eternally present. There is nothing esoteric about his message.

> *And after the Lord gave me brothers, no one showed me what I should do, but the Most High Himself revealed to me that I should live according to the form of the Holy Gospel.*[10]

Therefore "the rule and life" of the followers of Francis is simply "to observe the holy Gospel of our Lord Jesus Christ".[11] He encourages great love and reverence for "the words through which we are made and have been redeemed from death to life".[12] The Lord living in his

Church still continues to speak his "fragrant words" to us, for as Francis loves to recall, "they are spirit and life".[13] We find in them a life-giving presence. The Franciscan tradition is strong on the incarnational and the practical. Francis led the way in a wholehearted interiorising of the Word that bore fruit in life.

> *For he was no deaf hearer of the gospel; rather*
> *he committed everything he heard to his excel-*
> *lent memory and was careful to carry it out to*
> *the letter.*[14]

For the Gospel only becomes living for us when we take it into our lives. He is particularly drawn to the Sermon on the Mount and the new vision of humanity revealed there. The Gospel passage most alluded to in his writings is not any of the famous hard sayings of Jesus but the "golden rule" of human relationships: "Always treat others as you would like them to treat you" (Matthew 7:12). In his teaching, love, humility, fraternity, meekness, forgiveness, mutual service and courtesy are exalted to priority while programmes of ascetical exercises are lacking. When he lay dying, he reminded his brothers once again that the Gospel was always to be placed "ahead of other observances".[15]

It is clear that for Francis the Gospel is not simply some text book of instructions on the Christian life. Christ himself is the Gospel, the Good News of God for us. Living the Gospel means "to follow the teaching and footprints" of the Lord.[16] The Gospel is a way of seeing and a way of being in the world because of Christ. Jesus, poor and humble, captures the heart and imagination of Franciscans. It was said of Francis that "so thoroughly did the humility of the Incarnation and the charity of the Passion occupy his memory that he scarcely wanted to think about anything else".[17] His joy in the gift of Christ as saviour and brother overflows:

> *Oh, how holy, how loving, pleasing, humble, peaceful, sweet, lovable, and desirable above all things to have such a Brother and such a Son: our Lord Jesus Christ, Who gave up His life for His sheep.*[18]

The Spirit of the Lord

At the heart of the rule of life which Francis gave his brothers, he tells them that they should "desire above all things to have the Spirit of the Lord and His holy manner of working".[19] It is this emphasis on the essential role and action of the Holy Spirit in the Christian life that makes Franciscan spirituality a baptismal spirituality, a passionate consciousness of the divine gift already received. We journey to God with God and in God. For Francis, the secret of sanctity is the secret of surrender to the Holy Spirit. Like creation, salvation is not what we achieve but what we receive. We come to the Lord always by his "grace alone".[20] Our task, under grace, is to remain open to the Spirit's "holy manner of working". In declaring that the Holy Spirit was the true Minister General of the Order, he was stressing that our primary obedience must be to the indwelling Spirit.[21]

This leads to the sense of liberty evident in the Franciscan approach to the Christian life. There is a reverence for and sensitivity to the mystery of grace present in each person in whom "divine inspiration" is at work.[22] Thus there is a great deal of freedom given in the *Rule*. Primarily it is describing a life, not setting down regulations. The uniqueness of the vocation and gifts of each person is celebrated. Francis's letter to his companion Brother Leo, who was struggling over some decision, is a classic example of this spiritual freedom. Leo is told:

> *In whatever way it seems best to you to please the Lord God and to follow His footprints and His poverty, do this with the blessing of God and my obedience.*[23]

In his teaching about following the Lord, Francis never uses the word imitate. By the gift of the Spirit, we participate interiorly in the life of the risen Jesus, not simply imitate Him externally. Francis calls to an ever-deeper participation in the life of the Christ by the grace of the Spirit. If Jesus is the Way then the Spirit is the Fire that propels us on the path to God. In a prayer composed towards the end of his life, a synthesis of his Christian vision, Francis prays that:

> *inwardly cleansed, interiorly enlightened, and inflamed by the fire of the Holy Spirit, may we be able to follow in the footprints of your beloved Son, our Lord Jesus Christ, and by your grace alone, may we make our way to You, Most High.*[24]

In Francis's own life, the grace of the stigmata was the culmination of a process of profound identification with Christ. We are given a glimpse of the level of intimacy, the depth of communion to which we are invited. The wounds on Francis's flesh were the external signs of an inner union brought about by the Holy Spirit.

A Dwelling Place for God

Francis recognises that submitting our lives to the Spirit of the Lord is never easy. It calls for continual conversion and discernment. He constantly points to the heart. He warns us to be "very careful of the malice and the subtlety of Satan" who tries to capture the heart in whatever way he can. He:

> wishes that a man not raise his mind and heart to God. And as he roams about, he wishes to ensnare the heart of a person under the guise of some reward or help, and to snuff out our memory of the word and precepts of the Lord, and wishes to blind the heart of a person through worldly affairs and concerns.[25]

For Francis, the basic question of the spiritual journey is: what absorbs the desires of the heart? Francis recognises that we have the freedom to "insult" or even "quench" the Spirit.[26] Influenced by the theology of St Paul, he frequently refers to the dichotomy and struggle between *the Spirit of the Lord* and *the spirit of the flesh* (see Galatians 5:16–26). Flesh here does not refer to the body but to the deep self-centred tendency present in every human heart that resists the divine invasion. So it is not so much individual acts of sin that he focuses on but the drive to egocentrism, the refusal to be creature, which is at the root of all our estrangement from God and others.

This is where penance comes in. It is meant to create the inner space in which the Spirit has freedom within us. It is not a question of mastering anything but of being mastered by the Spirit of the Lord. All growth in discipleship is growth in yielding to the Spirit's dynamic action. It means to come before God without defences, without compromise, fully available, empty for God. The struggle is real; the choice stark. Francis is ruthless when it comes to discerning the movements of the heart, the source of our thoughts, words and deeds. He points out the authentic signs of the Spirit's presence.

> *For the spirit of the flesh desires and is eager to have words, but cares little to carry them out. And it does not seek a religion and holiness in the interior but it wishes and desires to have a religion and holiness outwardly apparent to people. . . . But the Spirit of the Lord wishes the flesh to be mortified and despised, worthless and rejected. And it strives for humility and patience, and the pure and simple and true peace of the spiritual person. And above all it longs for the divine fear and the divine wisdom and the divine love of the Father, and of the Son, and of the Holy Spirit.*[27]

The goal of this transforming work of the Spirit within us is a pure heart, a heart that can truly be a home for God. When Francis heard the Lord speak from the Cross of San Damiano, he was told, "Go, rebuild my house; as you see, it is all being destroyed".[28] Initially he believed the command referred to the ruined little church in which he prayed and at once he began to rebuild it. Later he realised that his vocation related to the Church, the universal house of God, and also to each Christian called to be the dwelling place of God. Francis frequently alludes to Christ's promise: "We will come to him and make our dwelling place in him" (John 14:23). Francis develops wonderfully the Gospel truth that every faithful disciple is mother of the Lord (see Matthew 12:50).

> *We are mothers, when we carry Him in our heart and body through divine love and a pure and sincere conscience and when we give birth to Him through His holy manner of working, which shine before others as an example.*[29]

For Francis, Mary is present in the heart of the Church as an abiding mystery. She is, in Francis's rich phrase, "the virgin made church".[30] All that the Church is called to be as bearer of the Good News was lived fully by Mary. She gave birth physically to the Christ whom we are called to bring forth spiritually. In a unique way, Mary is "the spouse of the Holy Spirit".[31] But Francis recognised that the Spirit of the Lord also overshadows each Christian bringing the Word to life within them.

The mystery of the Word made flesh continues in our lives to the extent that we are receptive to the action of the Spirit. Francis makes an impassioned plea that we seek this pure heart, this worthy home for God, with our whole being because this is what God "desires above all things".

> *In the holy love which is God I beg all my brothers as they overcome every obstacle and put aside every care and anxiety, to strive as best they can to serve, love, honour, and adore the Lord God with a clean heart and a pure mind, for this is what He desires above all things. And let us make a home and dwelling place for Him Who is the Lord God Almighty, Father and Son and Holy Spirit.*[32]

Within the Holy Church

Franciscan life is rooted firmly in the Catholic Church. We belong wholeheartedly to the Church that, even with its weaknesses and failings, is still the privileged place of encounter with the risen Christ. Francis always refers to *sancta ecclesia* — the holy Church. He himself promised "obedience and reverence to the Lord Pope".[33] He wanted his followers to be "always submissive and prostrate at the feet of the same holy Church and steadfast in the Catholic faith".[34] The dream of Pope Innocent III in which he saw a tottering Lateran Basilica, the Pope's cathedral church, being propped up by "a poor little man, small and scorned . . . with his own back bent so that it would not fall" has always been seen as a symbol of the Franciscan mission to work for the ongoing building up and renewal of the Church.[35]

In particular, for Francis, the Church is the place of the Eucharist:

> *Let the whole of mankind tremble, the whole world shake and the heavens exult when Christ the Son of the living God is present on the altar in the hands of the priest.*[36]

For Francis, the Eucharist is the reality of Christ among us present in littleness and hiddenness, just as he was in the womb of Mary:

> *See, every day He humbles Himself just as He did when He came from His heavenly throne into the Virgin's womb; everyday He comes to us in a humble form.*[37]

Francis was overwhelmed by this divine self-giving. "Look, brothers, at the humility of God!"[38] But this devotion was not limited to silent contemplation. The Eucharist is a way of being. It is the model and source of strength for the outpouring of our own lives. It is the way of Jesus who came and comes not in majesty but in lowliness.

> *Therefore hold back nothing of yourselves for yourselves so that He Who gives Himself totally to you may receive you totally.*[39]

Thus the image of the Lord washing the apostles' dirty feet is very important in Franciscan thought. It is recognised as a powerful, lived parable central to the Gospel. Francis was awestruck: the Creator kneels before His creatures! Loving, humble service is a way of life, the core of all relations within the Christian community.

> *And no one should be called Prior, but all gen-*
> *erally should be called Friars Minor. And the*
> *one should wash the feet of the others.*[40]

The Way of Simplicity

Francis's journey from rich young man seeking worldly glory to a poor follower of the poor Christ was eventful and lengthy. But at the end of his life, when Francis reflected on his journey of conversion he focused on one key element: his encounter with the lepers. Francis writes in *The Testament*, completed shortly before he died:

> *The Lord granted me, Brother Francis, to begin*
> *to do penance in this way: While I was in sin, it*
> *seemed very bitter to me to see lepers. And the*
> *Lord Himself led me among them and I had*
> *mercy upon them. And when I left them that*
> *which seemed bitter to me was changed into*
> *sweetness of soul and body; and afterwards I*
> *lingered a little and left the world.*[41]

Francis's meeting with the most rejected members of his society changed his life. He never forgot that the turning point in his conversion was not some great mystical experience in a lonely cave. It came when he showed love to the lepers and cared for their broken, despised bodies. We find the Lord in a particular way in the weak and poor. All our spiritual experiences must be judged by the fruit of mercy. This embrace of the leper remains an essential icon within Franciscan spirituality. It continues to be a "dangerous memory" that inspires many to action.

It is often forgotten in the romanticism of the Franciscan story that there was a definite social dimension to Francis's conversion. After this encounter with the lepers, Francis said he "left the world". That is, he opted out of the social system he had been so much a part of as a wealthy cloth merchant in that age of wool. When someone joined Francis, he disenfranchised himself. Life in the movement meant a real exodus from society, not simply a spiritualised one. While continuing to love and serve, they refuse to accept society on its own terms. They respond to the prevailing climate of greed and injustice by proposing a different kind of life, a counter-culture based on the Gospel. Among other things, this conversion involves a rejection of the class system of the day and a new set of relationships. Francis tells his followers that:

> *they must rejoice when they live among people who are considered to be of little worth and who are looked down upon, among the poor and the powerless, the sick and the lepers, and the beggars by the wayside.*[42]

Francis chose to live among the poor because Christ "was a poor man and a transient and lived on alms, He and the Blessed Mother and His disciples".[43] Society looks very different from that position.

The title Francis gave his Order reflects this social option. The brothers are *fraters minores*, lesser brothers. They adopt a very precise social position after the example of Christ and in order to reach everyone more freely and humbly. Francis was very definite on this point. Some of the more educated clerical friars wanted to take on a more respectable way of life by adopting one of the long-established rules for religious, but Francis was adamant.

> *My brothers! My brothers! God has called me by the way of simplicity and showed me the way of simplicity. I do not want you to mention any Rule, whether of St Augustine, or St Bernard, or St Benedict. . . . He wanted me to be a new fool in this world. God does not wish to lead us by any way other than this knowledge, but God will confound you by your knowledge and wisdom.*[44]

It is interesting that Francis wanted the foundational experience of being with the lepers to be shared by all who entered the Order.

> *At that time whenever nobles and commoners came to the Order, they were told, among other things, that they had to serve the lepers and stay in their houses.*[45]

Receiving All as Gift

This definite social option inherent in Franciscan spirituality has been more clearly recognised of late, and more fraternities live among the poor. But with the emphasis and the often controversial debate on poverty throughout Franciscan history, there is the constant risk of losing sight of what is essential in Franciscan Gospel poverty. In the writings of St Francis, three-quarters of those passages that treat of poverty concern spiritual, interior poverty; the rest deal with material poverty. The key to grasping the Franciscan understanding of Christian poverty is the term used often by Francis: *sine proprio* — without anything of one's own. The person alienated from God appropriates the gifts of God, refusing to acknowledge the rights of the Creator, attempting to placing himself or herself as the centre of the world. The path of Gospel poverty, of *sine proprio*, is the way to repair the sin of injustice that is at the root of the Fall from grace at the dawn of creation. Christ, poor and humble, dying naked on the Cross, overcame the consequences of this refusal to be trusting creature before the loving Creator. Disappropriation is the unique characteristic of Franciscan poverty. It means to freely, joyfully acknowledge the source of all good, the Most High God.

> *Let us refer all good to the most high and supreme Lord God, and acknowledge that every good is His, and thank Him for everything, He from Whom all good things come.*[46]

Francis uses words like property, possession, wealth
and ownership about every type of goods, not only material things but spiritual, intellectual, legal, even virtues and natural endowments. *Sine proprio* is the
fundamental element in our relations with God, our inner self and with others. The Admonition on anger over
sin shows how possessing can take many forms:

> *Nothing should upset the servant of God except
> sin. And no matter how another person may
> sin, if the servant of God lets himself become
> angry and disturbed because of this, and not
> because of love, he stores up the guilt for him-
> self. That servant of God who does not become
> angry or upset at anything lives justly and
> without anything of his own [sine proprio]. And
> he is blessed who does not keep anything for
> himself, rendering to Caesar what is Caesar's,
> and to God what is God's* [Matthew 22:21].[47]

Of course, material poverty and simplicity of life are a
part of Franciscan spirituality, and are perennial challenges for all who follow the way of Francis of Assisi.
But they must be a sign, the sacrament of this deep inner attitude. Material poverty is not an absolute, only
love of God and others can be that. Love is the purest
expression of interior poverty. It is interesting that in
his writings, Francis forbids the use of money, yet in the
case of the care of the sick brothers and the lepers it is,
at times, permissible.[48] Without true interior humility
and genuine love, the focus on poverty can become a
source of fanaticism and self-righteousness, a danger

not always avoided in Franciscan history. Without poverty of spirit there is no abundance of God. The line from *The Praises of God* that Francis composed on Mount La Verna after receiving the stigmata expresses beautifully the truth that is the heart of Franciscan poverty: "You are all our riches. You are enough for us."[49]

Sent into the Whole World

There is nothing inward looking about Franciscan spirituality. In a letter written to the friars near the end of his life Francis reiterates the missionary element of the Franciscan charism:

> *Give praise to Him since He is good and exalt Him by your deeds for He has sent you into the entire world for this reason: that in word and deed you might given witness to His voice and bring everyone to know that there is no one who is all-powerful except Him.*[50]

The ideas of being sent, of itinerancy, and of being available for mission are constant in the Franciscan tradition. In a famous passage in the allegorical work *The Sacred Exchange between Saint Francis and Lady Poverty*, Lady Poverty asks Francis and his brothers to show her their enclosure.

> *Taking her to a certain hill, they showed her all the world they could see and said: "This, Lady, is our enclosure."*[51]

The enclosure has traditionally been seen as the symbol of the contemplative life and the search for God. When Franciscans state that the world is their enclosure they are saying that it is in the midst of the earthy and at times messy drama of the human condition they encounter the living God. Franciscan mysticism does not imply withdrawal from the world but rather the commitment to be a Gospel presence in it.

Above all, this presence involves the witness of life. Francis clearly wished his followers to be evangelists. But the quality of their Christian lives has priority in the work of evangelisation. In his *Rule*, Francis tells the friars how they are to travel about the world, simply as brothers, little and humble.

> *I counsel, admonish and exhort my brothers in the Lord Jesus Christ, that, when they go about the world, they do not quarrel, or fight with words, or judge others; rather let them be meek, peaceful and unassuming, gentle and humble, speaking courteously to everyone as is becoming.*[52]

Before any words are spoken, their lives must be the message. He writes: "All the brothers should preach by their deeds".[53] Again and again he uses the phrase *verbo et exemplo* — by word and example. And the deeds are more essential than the words because life is always more powerful than language.

Hospitality, flowing from the vision of fraternity, is a core Franciscan value. As brothers and sisters, neither doors nor hearts should be closed to anyone. This is where poverty and fraternity meet. The one who is radically poor, who has rid his heart of the desires to possess and control, those desires that prevent trust and openness, only such a person can be free to be brother or sister to others. Francis writes:

> *Whoever comes to them, friend or foe, rogue or robber, should be received with kindness.*[54]

A key task is to create that welcoming space where the grace of God can be recognised and experienced. The friendship and table fellowship used so powerfully by the Lord to welcome back those considered outside the bounds are the model. Francis wanted fraternal life to reveal the Gospel in action and to be a mode of evangelisation.

This reliance on fraternal witness of life reveals a great trust in the grace of God at work in each human heart and in simple human encounters. Francis understood that men and women cannot be harangued or bullied into the Kingdom of God. What condemnation, angry words and accusation cannot do, gentle kindness, courtesy and humble patience can achieve. The Franciscan approach must be to draw by attraction: "Let them show that they are joyful in the Lord and cheerful and truly gracious".[55] When sending out the friars to sing *The Canticle of Brother Sun* in the piazzas, he compared the Lord's servants with minstrels or troubadours, men often frowned upon in Church circles at that time:

> *What are the servants of God if not His min-*
> *strels, who must move people's hearts and lift*
> *them up to spiritual joy?* [56]

It has been said that Francis "walked the world as the Pardon of God". It was as if people could glimpse in him how much they were accepted and cherished by God, and so were given the courage to be reconciled. After a chapter meeting, in words of abiding relevance, Francis spoke of the necessity to manifest in our lives the compassion of God and the beauty of the Gospel:

> *As you announce peace with your mouth, make*
> *sure that greater peace is in your hearts. Let*
> *none be provoked to anger or scandal through*
> *you, but may everyone be drawn to peace, kind-*
> *ness, and harmony through your gentleness. For*
> *we have been called to this: to heal the wounded,*
> *bind up the broken, and recall the erring.* [57]

The Gospel of Peace

Francis's meeting with the Sultan Malik el-Kamil, the leader of the Muslim armies, continues to be an event that informs and influences Franciscan living. The Fifth Crusade had been called by Pope Innocent III. Francis had gone with some of his brothers to Syria in 1219. There he had witnessed the terrible brutality of the capture of the Saracen city of Damietta. He then did something that was considered insane. Along with Brother Illuminato he left the Crusaders' camp, crossed no-man's-land, and got to meet, indeed stayed with, the great sultan. [58] It is difficult for us to understand the radical nature of Francis's action and the impact it had on men on both sides of the battle line. It was totally against the thinking of the age. There was at that time in the Church a mysticism of war against the infidel. But Francis went to the Saracens' camp "fortified only with the shield of faith. He said: 'I am a Christian!'"[59] After some time there the sultan had him led back to the Christian camp:

> *with all reverence and security. At the end he said to Francis: "Pray for me, that God may deign to reveal to me the law and faith which is most pleasing to Him".*[60]

The ivory horn given by the sultan to Francis, kept today in Assisi, is the symbol of fraternal dialogue, a sign of the way of Franciscan mission. Francis has been described as the man "with the unarmed heart". His peaceful offensive was not so much an unsuccessful attempt at conversion as the defeat of the Crusaders' mentality and a manifestation of the authentic Gospel spirit. So it was for good reason that in 1986, Pope John Paul II chose Assisi as the venue for the historic gathering of world religious leaders. By his prophetic gesture in meeting with the sultan, Francis challenged the Church to ponder more deeply the profound implications of the revelation of God in Christ.

In chapter sixteen of *The Earlier Rule* Francis gives the great statement on the Franciscan mission.[61] The *Rule of the Friars Minor* is the first rule in the Church to include a chapter on missionary evangelisation. In it are set forth the principles we see in action in Francis's encounter with the sultan. This passage concentrates on how the brothers are to conduct themselves among the Saracens and other unbelievers. Firstly, the friars are sent not *to* but *among* these people, and their primary task is to "live spiritually" among them, that is, under the guidance and grace of the Spirit of the Lord. They are to do this in two ways: "One way is not to engage in arguments and disputes." Francis had little faith in the power of arguments to change the human heart. Rather, they should "be subject to every human creature for God's sake". (see 1 Peter 2:13). The friars should be *minores*, little brothers among these people. They are to refuse all claims to power. Such an approach makes one vulnerable to others and open to suffering; it is the way of Christ. The friars are to state why they so live by acknowledging "that they are Christians". Francis makes clear that this humble submission is to be done "for God's sake". On human terms, it is complete folly. The second way of living "spiritually" is to proclaim the Word of God. But they should do this only "when they see that it pleases the Lord". We are not masters of the Word but first and foremost listeners. We must be sensitive to the voice of the Spirit in each situation. The Word of God needs a soil that has been prepared. This text is the guide for those Franciscan men and women who live simple, contemplative lives of witness among the peoples of various Muslim countries today.

The Fraternity of Creation

Franciscan fraternity would not be totally complete if it did not also open itself in a truly cosmic union with all creatures. In the sources we have for the life of Francis, there are many stories that tell of his deep delight in creation and of his extraordinary relationship with and affection for creatures. We have him preaching to birds, encountering the wolf of Gubbio, freeing doves being brought to the market, stories about crickets, rabbits and lambs. In fact, a whole zoo turns up in the pages of the Franciscan sources! Now while some of these stories may be embellished, there is no doubt that Francis was able to relate to all sorts of creatures in a way that astonished his contemporaries.

This fraternal approach to creation is a distinctive element of Franciscan spirituality, one that is particularly attractive to people today. But we need to be clear that Francis was not a sentimental romantic whose idea of being close to nature was fresh air and frolics in the forests. In *The Canticle of Brother Sun*, Francis praises not just fair weather but also all kinds of weather; he who knew what it was to suffer terribly in his mountain hermitages during cold and wet days.

> *Praise to You, my Lord, through Brother Wind, and through the air, cloudy and serene, and every kind of weather through which You give sustenance to Your creatures.*[62]

In the account of the sermon to the birds at Bevagna, there is a mixture of attractive and not so attractive

birds, including crows and jackdaws.[63] Francis was not
naïve about nature. It is not idealised.

In his canticle, he sings of Brother Sun and Sister
Moon, of Brothers Wind and Fire and Sister Water. It
has been said that if he was alive today he would update
his canticle to include Brother DNA and Sister Nuclear
Fusion. Francis also spoke to the friars of Brother worm
and of his Sisters, the flowers and the birds. These titles
are more profound than just pleasant poetic ideas.
Rather, they flow from a God-given insight into what it
means to be creature. All creatures are united in the
depths of their being by the fact of being creature. As a
creature, Francis knew his existence was pure, un-
earned gift. To fully and joyfully accept the truth than
one is creature is a core dimension of Franciscan spirituality. The source and foundation of our being is not in
ourselves. In this fundamental poverty of being creature, there is equality. The human person has no more
claim to intrinsic being than a daisy or cat, a star or
stone. The unique role given to humanity in creation
and redemption is as completely a gift of God as is the
role of every creature. The only reason for anything to
exist is the free self-giving love of God. Utterly dependent, creation is divinely gifted.

Francis readily acknowledged his ties with the rest of
creation in its dependence upon the Creator. "Praised be
You, my Lord, with all Your creatures".[64] He grasped
that creation is now! In God we exist. At every instant
we are willed into existence by His love. Francis exhorts
his brothers to love fully the God "who gave and *gives* to

all of us our whole body, our whole soul, our whole life".[65] So the Franciscan vision sees our relationship with creation not primarily as one of possession or utility but rather one of shared life and companionship. The notion of our stewardship of creation, misunderstood as it has been, has tended to absent God from the picture, giving human beings full licence to use creation as they like for their own benefit, with disastrous consequences.

So many stories capture this vision of Francis. When cutting wood, the friars were not to cut down the whole tree "so that it might have hope of sprouting again".[66] Practical utility should not dominate our thinking. A definite area of the garden was to be left fallow for wild flowers and herbs "so that in their proper times the greenness of the grass and the beauty of the flowers might announce the beauty of the Father of all things".[67] Francis has a special reverence for the Sun and for Brother Fire:

> *For we are all like blind people, and the Lord lights up our eyes through these two creatures. Because of this, we must always praise the glorious Creator for these and for His other creatures which we use each day.*[68]

When Francis found an abundance of flowers "he preached to them and invited them to praise the Lord as though they were endowed with reason".[69] The image of the wolf of Gubbio, which had previously terrorised the people, sitting peacefully at Francis's feet is a foreshadowing of the universal reconciliation, promised by

Isaiah, when the lamb and the lion will lie down together (see Isaiah 11:6).[70]

Francis saw the same things that we see but he saw
them in a different way:

> *In an extraordinary manner, a manner never
> experienced by others, he discerned the hidden
> things of nature with his sensitive heart, as one
> who has already escaped into the freedom of the
> glory of the sons of God.*[71]

Grace opens our eyes so that we can rejoice in the majesty and loveliness of the Creator revealed in His
handiwork:

> *In every work of the artist Francis praised the
> Artist. Whatever he found in things made, he re-
> ferred to the Maker. He rejoiced in all the works
> of the hands of the Lord and saw behind things
> pleasant to behold their life-giving reason and
> cause. In beautiful things he saw Him who is
> Beauty itself. All things were good to him. They
> cried out to him: "He who made us is the best!"
> Through his footprints impressed upon creation
> Francis followed his Beloved everywhere. He
> made for himself from all things a ladder by
> which to come even to God's throne.*[72]

Creation itself is a revelation of the divine. Creation is
God's first word, a visible word to us. Franciscan spirituality tells us if we walk through this world as brothers
and sisters, alive to the reality of our common creature-
hood, then indeed *the book of creation* is opened for us.

Notes

---

[1] *2 Celano*, 12. The many legenda and chronicles, both Franciscan and others, that record the details of the life of St Francis are found in Armstrong et al., 1999, 2000, 2001.

[2] *The Praises of God*, 4, 5.

[3] *The Second Letter to the Faithful*, 62.

[4] *The Earlier Rule*, 23:9.

[5] Op. cit., 23:11.

[6] Ibid.

[7] *The Later Rule*, 5:2.

[8] *The Rule for Hermitages*, 3.

[9] *The Earlier Rule*, 23:8.

[10] *The Testament*, 14.

[11] *The Later Rule*, 1:1.

[12] *A Letter to the Clergy*, 3.

[13] *The First Letter to the Faithful*, 2:19, 20.

[14] *1 Celano*, 22.

[15] *The Major Legend*, 14:5.

[16] *The Earlier Rule*, 1:1.

[17] *1 Celano*, 84.

[18] *The First Letter to the Faithful*, 1:13.

[19] *The Later* Rule, 10:8.

[20] *A Letter to the Entire Order*, 52. Although Francis considered himself "ignorant and unlettered", quite a number of

his writings have come down to us. The translations used
here are from Armstrong and Brady, 1982.

21 See *2 Celano*, 193.

22 See *The Earlier Rule*, 2:1; *The Later Rule*, 12:1; *The Form
    of Life*, 1.

23 *A Letter to Brother Leo*, 3.

24 *A Letter to the Entire Order*, 51, 52.

25 *The Earlier Rule*, 22:19, 20.

26 See *A Letter to the Entire Order*, 18; *The Later Rule*, 5:2.

27 *The Earlier Rule*, 17:11–16.

28 *2 Celano*, 10.

29 *The First Letter to the Faithful*, 1:10.

30 *The Salutation of the Blessed Virgin Mary*, 1.

31 *The Office of the Passion*, antiphon.

32 *The Earlier Rule*, 22:26, 27.

33 *The Later Rule*, 1:2.

34 Op. cit., 12:4.

35 *The Major Legend*, 3:9.

36 *A Letter to the Entire Order*, 26.

37 *Admonitions*, 1:16, 17.

38 *A Letter to the Entire Order*, 28.

39 Op. cit., 29.

40 *The Earlier Rule*, 6:3, 4.

41 *The Testament*, 1–3.

42 *The Earlier Rule*, 9:2.

43 Op. cit., 9:5.

44 *The Assisi Compilation*, 18.

45 Op. cit., 9.

46 *The Earlier Rule*, 17:17.

47 *The Admonitions*, 11.

48 See *The Earlier Rule*, 8:3, 10.

49 *The Praises of God*, 4.

50 *A Letter to the Entire Order*, 9.

51 *The Sacred Exchange*, 63.

52 *The Later Rule*, 3:10, 11.

53 *The Earlier Rule*, 17:3.

54 Op. cit., 7:14.

55 Op. cit., 7:16.

56 *The Assisi Compilation*, 83.

57 *The Legend of the Three Companions*, 58.

58 See *The Major Life*, 9:7–9.

59 Jacques de Vitry, *Historia Occidentalis*, 14.

60 Ibid.

61 *The Earlier Rule*, 16.

62 *The Canticle of Brother Sun*, 6.

63 *1 Celano*, 58.

64 *The Canticle of Brother Sun*, 3.

[65] *The Earlier Rule*, 23:8.

[66] *2 Celano*, 165.

[67] Ibid.

[68] *The Assisi Compilation*, 83.

[69] *1 Celano*, 81.

[70] See *The Little Flowers of St Francis*, 21.

[71] *1 Celano*, 81

[72] *2 Celano*, 165.

References

Armstrong, A. and Brady, I. (1982), *Francis and Clare: The Complete Works*, New York: Paulist Press.

Armstrong, R., Hellmann, J.A.W., and Short, W. (eds.), (1999), *Francis of Assisi: Early Documents. Volume I, The Saint*, New York: New City Press.

— (2000), *Francis of Assisi: Early Documents. Volume II, The Founder*, New York: New City Press.

— (2001), *Francis of Assisi: Early Documents. Volume III, The Prophet*, New York: New City Press.

Further Reading

Boff, L. (1982), *Saint Francis: A Model for Human Liberation*, New York: Crossroad.

Rotzetter, A., Van Dijk, W.C. and Matura, T. (1994), *Gospel Living: Francis of Assisi, Yesterday and Today*, St Bonaventure, NY: Franciscan Institute.

Short, W. (1989), *The Franciscans*, Wilmington, DL: Glazier.

7

IGNATIAN SPIRITUALITY

Joseph Veale, SJ

I do not think St Ignatius would be comfortable with either word in the phrase "Ignatian Spirituality". "Spirituality", the word, is bloodless, often too self-conscious, artificial, cut off from the noises and smells of God's world. And as for "Ignatian", well, he would say that Christian teachers do not stand on their own. They take their place in the river of tradition and all they do is to try to live the Gospel. There is one way — the Way, the Truth and the Life. God works in a great variety of ways; but what is common to all spiritualities is larger than the differences. St Ignatius will have been wryly amused (or exasperated) by Jesuits who have magnified his importance.

St Ignatius lived at a time (1491–1556) when everything was in flux. He straddled the late mediaeval world and the new early modern world. He belonged to both. He is modern in his trust in experience.

He has been given to say (by Karl Rahner, who has Ignatius speak to the Jesuits of the late 1970s) what his purpose was:

> *I should now explain more clearly for you re-*
> *pressed atheists of today how it is possible to*
> *meet God directly. . . . As you know my great*
> *desire was to "help souls". . . to tell people about*
> *God and his grace and about Jesus Christ . . . so*
> that their freedom could become the freedom of
> God . . . *I was convinced in Loyola and then de-*
> *cisively in Manresa, that I had a direct encoun-*
> *ter with God. This was the experience I longed*
> *to communicate to others.*[1]

Freedom and the experience of God. How to enable persons to grow into more freedom, wherever they are on the road to God, indecisively good or boldly sinful, the devout and the alienated, misbelievers or unbelievers or the worrying pious. In that interior freedom, God would make himself known.

He jotted down the things he had found in his experience to be of help in his own growth: "He told me that he had not made up the exercises all at once, but that when he found some things were helpful to himself, he thought they might be helpful to others, and so he put them in writing . . ."[2] These "some exercises" became what we know as the *Spiritual Exercises*. They were the jottings of a layman and for many years it was as a layman that he helped others to find their way forward on the way to God.

Where He Came From

Ignatius was Basque, a youngest son who had to make his way in the world, on the bottom rungs of a ladder who might well have ended up being a great name in the world; he had the makings of a statesman. He was a courtier, a part-time soldier when there was need, given to the sexual sins and the touchy honour of a *hidalgo*, with a record in the police reports. He was pious in the conventional way of his home and of a court influenced by the spiritual renewal of the time, the first two decades of the 1500s. He knew where he was going. Then, in full career, he was thrown. Dislocation and falling flat on your face is a great eye-opener. A broken leg in a small local fight sent him back to his Basque home.

He was full of contradictions. He had begun to get a reputation for diplomatic shrewdness. He was also filled with a romantic imagination that dreamed of chivalry and winning the hand of a princess. While his leg was being broken again and re-set to serve his vanity, they could not find the romances of the time to while the time away, but gave him the only books in the place, the *Legenda Aurea,* lives of the saints, and Ludolph of Saxony's *Vita Christi.* Later, it would be written of him:

> . . . *as for the elections (that is the process of discerning God's will through observing the interior movements of consolation and desolation) . . . he had drawn them from that variety of*

*spirit and thoughts which he had had when he
was in Loyola, when he was still ill from his leg.*

His daydreaming could go on for hours, fantasising
about doing great deeds in the service of a great lady.
Those fantasies consoled him, but left him afterwards
empty and unsettled. His dreaming of imitating the
saints, especially his admiration for St Dominic and St
Francis, consoled him:

> *. . . always proposing to himself difficult and la-
> borious things. And as he was proposing these,
> it seemed to him easy to accomplish . . .*

The succession of such diverse thoughts, either of
worldly deeds or of the deeds of God that came to his
imagination, lasted for a long time. Yet there was a difference. When he thought of going to Jerusalem bare-
foot, eating nothing but herbs and undergoing all the
other rigours that he saw the saints endured, not only
was he consoled, but even after putting these thoughts
aside, he remained content and happy. He felt within
himself a very great desire to serve Our Lord. He began
to marvel at the difference and to reflect on it. Little by
little, he came to realise the difference between the spirits that moved him, one from the devil, the other from
God.

A Process of Conversion

But he had much to learn and much in the subtle pride of his devious spirit that needed to be purified. When he set out, unaware of where God might be leading him, he:

> . . . *was still blind though with a great desire to serve God in every way he knew. . . . He did not know what humility was or charity or patience or discretion to regulate and measure these virtues. His every intention was to do these external deeds because the saints had done them for the glory of God.*

A saintly Benedictine in the monastery of Montserrat helped him over three days to make his confession. On the eve of the feast of Our Lady in March in the year 1522, he "stripped off all his clothes and gave them to a poor man and dressed himself in his desired clothing" made of sackcloth, "loosely woven and very prickly and with a pilgrim's staff and a small gourd". He thought he would spend a few days in a local town, Manresa, "to note some things in his book that he carefully carried with him, and by which he was greatly consoled". He stayed there the best part of a year and his experience there transformed him (1523).

He lived by begging alms. He was "without any knowledge of the inward things of the spirit". His penances were excessive; he neglected his hygiene and appearance. He was thrown from delusory imaginings that gave him consolation into desolations that seem to have bordered on suicide. At times he found he took no joy in prayer or in hearing Mass or in any other prayer he said. He was tormented by scruples and found no help in the advice he sought. He felt disgust for the life he led and the desire to give it up overcame him.

> *He began to be frightened at these variations . . . and to say to himself: "What new life is this we're beginning now?"*

> *Through the lessons God had given him he now had some experience of the diversity of spirits and he now began to wonder about the means by which that spirit had come.*

This long purification ended in a series of contemplative experiences. They were of the Three Persons. Of the manner in which God created the world. Of "how Jesus Christ our Lord was there in the most holy sacrament". Of the humanity of Christ. And finally an understanding that seems to have contained and synthesised all the other intellectual visions:

> *While he was seated there by the river which was running deep, the eyes of his understanding began to be opened; though he did not see any vision, he understood and knew many things, both spiritual things and matters of faith and of learning. And this with so great an enlightenment that everything seemed new to him.*

The Desire to Help Souls

One of the first things he did was to wash. He cut his hair and nails. The bent of his union with God was now absorbed in the desire "to help souls". You needed to be ordinary, to be unremarkable.

What kind of God was this that he had encountered? God cares. He enters into the details of our lives, in all the facets of our experience. For St Ignatius, to be in union with God is to be in union with God as he is. God as he is is God active in his world. He is at work, labouring for us in the world, calling us to labour with him to complete his work on earth.

God in Christ is redeeming and sanctifying us through each other. What Saint Ignatius saw in Manresa was confirmed for him 15 years later, shortly after he was ordained priest, just outside Rome as he was walking from Venice towards the city, at a wayside shrine at La Storta. The Christ who calls us to be united with him in his labour is the Christ who is in the world carrying his cross now.

God then is in his world everywhere to be found. God's desire is to be known. His desire to find us is greater than our desire to find him. Ignatius wants the one making the *Exercises*, at the end, to "ponder with great affection how much God our Lord desires to give himself to me" (234).[3] God is found not by ignoring his world, but in it, through it and beyond it. We are united with God not by leaving his world behind or below but in it and through it. God gives himself to us not in spite of things but through them, not in spite of our body but through it, not by denying our humanity but through it, with all its shifting moods and revolts, its pig-headedness and blindness, its limits, our stupidities, our ambiguities, our darkness, our doubt and denials, our terrors and our violence and our addictions and ob-sessions, the traps we contrive for ourselves, our pains and impoverishment as well as our desires and aspira-tions and joys and splendours. The people he created are like that. He does not have any other kind to love and to work for and to work in and to work through.

Ignatius had no intention of founding an order. Friends at the University of Paris, circumstances and a long process of discernment led to that. The compan-ions who came together found that they shared the same experience of God, the same calling to get out on the streets, the roads, the ships. Their way of life was not something unimagined before. Saint Francis and Saint Dominic had sent men out on the roads of the world to preach the gospel. Yet the first companions with Ignatius, more radically than any before them, de-cloistered and de-monasticised that kind of life. Every-thing in their manner of living was to be a means to the end of helping souls. To be footloose, free, available and mobile, quick to respond to need, ready to improvise, free to risk failure, not fearing opprobrium, was what they wanted. That was the aspiration; the reality was often well short of the mark. They were not to belong to any place. It was said by one of them, "the principal and most characteristic dwelling for us is not in the house but on the road".

St Ignatius de-cloistered consecrated life more radically than before and he de-cloistered God. That would have been no great news to the Irish through the centuries, where every daily chore in the byre or the kitchen was calmly enclosed in a Gaelic prayer. But by the 1500s in Europe, God needed to be set free, to be given space and air. God unites himself with his people not only in holy places or spaces or in particular times or through particular kinds of activity, but in all things, in all situations, in all activities, in all relationships. In that way, in harmony with something that had always been there in Christian tradition, always implicit in the squalid reality of the incarnation, St Ignatius shifted the meaning of "prayer". God needs to be sought and found in prayer. He is not less to be found in washing one another's feet.

Contemplation and action, then, are not separate. One of his earlier followers, Jerome Nadal, more learned in theology, said that that way of life was "to be contemplative even in activity". But St Ignatius preferred to say simply "to find God in all things". Nadal's formulation could imply a disjunction between action and contemplation. St Ignatius's bent was always towards inclusion, reconciliation of opposites, synthesis rather than separation or opposition. The vocation was to be purely contemplative. For him, "to find God" was more than an awareness of God's presence in his world.

It indicated a particular experience of God in a process of contemplative decision. It entailed a habitual sensitivity to the leading of the Spirit in searching for God's will for his work in the world.

How to Find God in Life as it is?

How, in a life of fret and stress, is a person to find God? Because, of course, in the fret and stress God often is not found. Often he is not sought. You can be zealous for religion and not seek God. But for most people, there is simply the need to keep the show on the road, to make ends meet, to keep going, to survive. Good people find that the thicket of thorns in the parable chokes the seed. Quiet is needed to allow a person to get in touch with the hunger, to acknowledge the repressed desire. We can be hamstrung between fear and what we secretly know we need and want. If one were to ask St Ignatius how you might come to be able to live a life of labour and distraction and at the same time to grow through all that to be closer to God, he would almost certainly keep his counsel. He would be aware of the fears that paralyse desire. He would wonder how strong the desire was. He would feel compassion for the chains that bind a person's freedom. He would know of the subtle ways they are intertwined with the good.

But he might say: *Do you really mean it? Is that what you seriously want? Do you really want to be free? There are a thousand ways of going forward on the road. But here is one. Why not make what they call the* Spiritual Exercises?

The contemplative understandings he was given at Manresa were the substance of the ways in which he sought "to help souls", to help them so that their freedom might become the freedom of God. He insists that whoever is "giving" the *Exercises* is not to get in God's way but "to permit the Creator to deal directly with the creature and the creature with his Creator and Lord" (15). He was filled with respect for people's freedom. He wanted his disciples to be skilled in helping people to be given the freedom of the Spirit.

It seems it was from those Manresa experiences that he grasped the key to understanding the principle that underlay the fluctuating movements of consolation and desolation, of what he called the movements of the different spirits. It is what the tradition from Origen to Aquinas called *discretio*, the wisdom that sees what in the thickets of our motivations is of God and what is not. The heart of the *Exercises* is an apprenticeship to that free gift.

It was as a fruit of his contemplative experiences that he never saw creation apart from the Three Persons, God actively at work in created reality, our world in its concreteness and shiftiness, its limits and its ambiguities, its noise and its smell, its desires and aspirations, its sin and its disappointments, its heartbreak, its beauty and its nobility. Therefore, in his understanding,

Christ is central. God has taken on his own world. Jesus
is the Word *made flesh.*

Contemplating Jesus in the Gospel

Hence the importance of the Gospel and the importance
St Ignatius gave to contemplating Jesus in the Gospel.
In that, naturally, he was not original. An affectionate
and tender love of Jesus is Franciscan. Ignatius bor-
rowed from the living tradition as it was available to
him in his time. When it came to trying to find words to
convey the "understandings" he was given at Manresa
and later, he had to work within the limits of the language of the spiritual culture of his time. What seems to
have been original was that he took the simple way of
contemplating the events of the Gospel and transposed
that contemplation to the context of seeking God's will
in a process of discernment. Jesus in the Gospel is the
first criterion of discernment, of learning to be sensitive
to the leading of the Spirit, to being streetwise in notic-
ing the deceptions of the ego and of evil, of sensing
what is of God.

In the process of making the *Exercises*, Ignatius recommends a simple way of prayer, a way of being present with the whole self, body and mind and imagination and sensibility, to events in the Gospel, to the
"mysteries of the life of Our Lord". What he hoped was
that one would become absorbed in the reality of the
deeds and words of Jesus, that one would look and listen and wonder and touch and smell and taste, behold

the Persons, what they did and said, would assimilate and be assimilated to the "mystery". The one contemplating might be drawn through the icon of the scene or happening and beyond it into the mystery beyond the "mystery".

What St Ignatius presupposed in all that was that a person setting out for the first time on the road to a serious life of faith was being guided by someone experienced in the "manifold gifts of the Holy Spirit and the variety of graces through which He distributes His loving kindnesses". Such an experienced guide would be aware that "it is not much knowledge that fills and satisfies the soul but to savour and to taste the reality interiorly" (2). The one making the *Exercises* would in the day-by-day exchange with the other be shown that "where I find what I desire, there I quietly remain . . ." (76). That was Saint Ignatius's simple pedagogy, by which he opened the door upon the possibility of contemplation and the uniquely personal action of the Holy Spirit.

What is probably original in Ignatius is that in the *Exercises* he recommends a person who is praying an event in the Gospel to hear what the persons in the scene "say *or might say*", do or might do (123). The movement is from looking on at what is happening to participating in it, from what could be impersonal to what is personal and intimate. Ignatius was concerned to bring the Gospel reality into intimate and personal encounter with the contemporary reality of the person's own experience and history. How otherwise was Christ to become incarnate in greatly different cultures, in the faith and living of his people, in their world, in times unimagined in the 1500s?

It can be helpful to ponder the different ways in which God works in the spirit and life of different saints. The Catholic tradition, west and east, is rich in the variousness of the ways of apprehending God and coming close to him. St Ignatius himself, in his stern warning to what we would now call (or try to avoid calling) spiritual directors, says it is dangerous to "impose the same manner of life and way of prayer that has proved useful for themselves".[4] The Holy Spirit is the one teacher of prayer.

Helping People to Find God

So great was his reverence for the freedom of the person that he built into his *Exercises* a principle of adaptation. If he wanted to help individuals to grow, he found it helpful to know where they were on the road, where each one was coming from, what they were seeking, what was each one's mastering desire, how strong was his desire. Everything hinged on desire. The search for God is an encounter of two freedoms, of two desires: God's desire to give himself and the desire of the human heart for God. It is from that encounter that the dynamic of faith and grace goes forward. The *Exercises* are simply a way of entering into that dynamic of grace.

It has been said that to understand St Ignatius you have to see him as always in movement. He is always aware of process. Of growth. He took people where they were and explored with each one where they desired to go, suggesting what might help a person to the next step of growth, to where the action of God was calling them now. So you do not take a sinner already in despair at his own wretchedness and batter him with the demands of heroic sanctity. People are taken where they are and encouraged to aspire to what God enables them to manage. In these days, in dialogue with friends who are not Christian, with Moslem or Hindu or Jewish or innocent of God, you do not immediately deafen them with theology. People are tough and frail and God is gentle and strong. God has his times and he knows the capacity and pace of an individual. Someone who is asked to help is wise to know when to wait on God. What happens then is God's business.

St Ignatius is clear. That kind of prayer is best for each one where God desires to communicate himself more. It is for God to say how he desires to begin and develop that relationship. Faith and contemplation (the natural flowering of faith) are a reply to an invitation to relationship: "God sees and knows what is best for each one and, as he knows us all, he shows each the road to take. On our part we can with his grace seek and test the way forward in many different fashions, so that a person goes forward by that way which for them is the clearest and happiest and most blessed in this life."[5]

"We can seek and test the way forward in many different fashions." St Ignatius always preferred to proceed empirically. He was less at home with generalisations and rigid nostrums. To try to impose one's own way on the freedom of a person was harmful and the work of people:

> . . . *who neither knew nor understood the manifold gifts of the Holy Spirit and the variety of graces through which he distributes his loving kindness, giving each person their own special and particular graces, to some in one way and to others in another.*[6]

He would explore with a particular person in what direction their spirit was being moved, in what way God now seemed to desire to communicate himself. Or, in another of his idioms, where a person would more readily "find God". A sign would be a certain quality of "consolation", a term he has a particular range of meanings for, and not to be confused with "feeling good". Consolation might not be sensibly experienced or easily recognisable on the surface. His concern would be to see whether a particular way of praying (or seeming not to pray at all) opened the spirit more to the action of God. Was a person more open to God? Less self-preoccupied? More selfless in service? More loving? More unpretentious? Less rigid? More true? Showing effective signs of living the Gospel? More authentic in relating with others? Being drawn out of the self? Less subject to illusion? Growing in hope and love?

The heart of the *Exercises* is a process of testing the way forward, of being aware of the signs of God, of sensing the openings to finding the gifts of the Spirit (Gal. 5). In the fears that infest the spirit before serious decision, we hide ourselves from ourselves, hide ourselves from God. We run from the reality. Prayer and piety and good behaviour can be a comfortable stand-in for the living God. Good people can be beguiled by the attractions of security, of work, of learning, or of power. It is easy to build one's own kingdom, not God's. It has been brought home to us painfully how protecting the institution can take the place of the Gospel. Noble aspirations need scrutiny. It was St Ignatius's great concern to be always learning the ways in which "the enemy of our human nature" deceives the good under the appearance of good in seeking the good.

Desiring to be Placed with Christ

To enter more deeply into freedom, St Ignatius would point towards the freedom of Christ expressed in the Sermon on the Mount. That would move in the direction of desiring to be placed with Jesus in his experience of humility, of poverty, of rejection, a movement into the clarifying freedom of the Spirit (II Cor. 3:17). In no other way can we learn to escape the deceptions of the contrary spirit. The freedom of the Sermon on the Mount is not an achievement. It is not something to be done. It is something experienced as being given; that is, purely contemplative.[7] If it is not rooted in love and moved by love, it is best left aside.

Given something of that desire to enter into the mind of Christ, the workaday tasks and responsibilities and delights and frets, the enjoyments of life and its stress, the cares of family, of public life, of the kitchen or office or field or classroom or workbench, the pains of relationships and the laughter, whatever draws us out of ourselves to the needs of others, have been blessed and given the likeness of a sacrament through Jesus' words about washing another's feet. Whatever brings faith to life, whatever brings God to bear on everything else we experience, whatever draws our focus away from ourselves, whatever beauty or goodness so absorbs us as entirely to forget ourselves, whatever makes us more loving, all these can purify and illumine as much as prayer does. To be God-like is entirely to forget oneself. Whether that comes from a call to be absorbed only in God or by a life that engages one's love in others' needs is not for us to say.

How his Teaching was Changed

St Ignatius, with his instinctive sense of history, would expect us to have enriched and enlarged his insights, and to have corrected them with the experience of the intervening centuries and the resources of our contemporary culture and theologies. We need to understand something of the strange way in which his spiritual wisdom was turned on its head.

Within his lifetime, the *Exercises* came under attack for being too mystical. One of the Spanish Inquisitors accurately pinpointed those parts of the *Exercises* that were dangerous for that reason. He and Melchor Cano, one of the most learned and influential theologians of that time, feared the *Exercises* and Cano sought to meet Ignatius. He was persuaded that so dangerous a body as the Society of Jesus would be confirmed to be rotten fruit if the tree was found to be rotten. Ignatius invited him a few times to a meal. Cano wrote a report for the Pope to assure him that Ignatius was "full of wind", *habia mucho viento*, he was vainglorious, deluded, boastful of his spiritual gifts, rather too fond of his lineage and grand connections. He was a fraud.[8]

What was wrong with the *Exercises* was that they gave too much place to experience, to affectivity. They were not rational enough, underplaying the objective teaching of sound doctrine, above all giving prominence to the interior leading of the Spirit. People making the *Exercises* were not told what to think or what to do. The *Exercises* raised false expectations. The theological watchdogs were enraged at what was the central underlying assumption of the *Exercises*:

> *It is far better that the Creator and Lord himself communicate himself to the devout soul, embracing it to his love and praise, to allow the Creator to deal directly with the creature and the creature with its Creator and Lord (15).*

Cano's style of theology became the dominant orthodoxy in the Church for almost 400 years. Jesuits were
submitted to it and it was in that light that they interpreted the *Exercises*. That orthodoxy disallowed the
central insights of the *Exercises*. It became dominant in
Jesuit spirituality. The 16th-century fear of illuminism
was later reinforced after the condemnation of quietism
(1687) and of modernism (1907). Some Jesuits with experience of helping others quietly taught the older
Christian contemplative tradition, though not always
without being told to stop. It was only with the Vatican
Council II that there has been a freedom to return to a
more flexible and contemplative understanding of what
Ignatius was really on about. A bleak rationality and a
stifling of the mystical tradition in the church is one of
the factors that have led to Europe's apostasy from God.

Meanwhile God is always greater. It is His desire for
us to give Himself to us and to draw us in the direction
of being given over entirely to Him. People who are
called to labour are drawn into union with God when
their freedom allows God to use his gifts so that God
may be God in his world. Or God may build his kingdom by leaving his gifts unused. The freedom of the
Spirit is the deeper freedom to cling to nothing, not
even to the need to be effective. By one path or the
other, by God using his gifts or by leaving them unused,
the instrument is sanctified. That is God's business, not
ours. Let us think little of it. Meanwhile, there are tasks

to hand that are our business. Our goal is not to become holy but to be spent.

Notes

1. Rahner, K. (1979), "Ignatius Loyola Speaks to a Modern Jesuit" in *Ignatius of Loyola*, London: Collins, pp. 11, 14. Author's emphasis here and in subsequent quotations.

2. This quotation and the ones that follow are taken from the document that records a spoken account of "how God dealt with my soul". The translations quoted are from various sources. The text is found in Philip Endean's version in Munitiz, J.A. and Endean, P. (1996), *Personal Writings, Saint Ignatius of Loyola*, London: Penguin Classics. There, the page references are: 63, 15, 19, 20, 24, 27, 26.

3. Numbers in brackets refer to the paragraph numbering in the text of the *Spiritual Exercises*. For the text of the *Exercises*, see Munitiz and Endean, *op. cit.*, pp. 279–360.

4. Ribadeneira, P. de, *Vita Ignatii Loyolae*, Monumenta Historica Societatis Iesu, Vol.93, p. 854.

5. Munitiz and Endean, *op. cit.*, p. 204. Letter of 20 September 1548, from Rome to St Francis Borgia.

6. Ribadeneira, *op. cit.*, p. 854.

7. "Contemplative". The idiom used by St Ignatius was *de arriba, desursum*, meaning "from above". We find it hard any longer to use the word "mystic", or "mystical", given the media's widespread misuse of the term to refer to any vaguely religious manifestations of the irrational. The older, more traditional, term, "contemplative", is better. "Mystical" here, like "contemplative", refers to "the aspect of passivity that is found again and again in every interior life". Joseph de Guibert, "Mystique", *RAM*, 7 [1926].

8. O'Reilly, T. (1995), "Melchor Cano's *Censura y paracer contra el Instituto de los Padres Jesuitas*: A Transcription of the British Museum Manuscript" in *From Ignatius Loyola to John of the Cross: Spirituality and Literature in Sixteenth-Century Spain*, London: Variorum.